T0021682

LOGAN'S WAR
AGAINST STAGE IV

A WARRIOR'S BATTLE TO VICTORY

A SHLEIGH SNYDER

authorHOUSE®

AuthorHouse™
1663 Liberty Drive
Bloomington, IN 47403
www.authorhouse.com
Phone: 1 (800) 839-8640

Published by AuthorHouse   01/11/2016

ISBN: 978-1-5049-7286-4 (sc)
ISBN: 978-1-5049-7283-3 (hc)
ISBN: 978-1-5049-7284-0 (e)

Library of Congress Control Number: 2016900373

Print information available on the last page.

Dedication

To my Loganator, who has shown me strength I never knew I had as a mother. I am so proud that God chose me to be your mommy. Your perseverance and resilience are lessons to us all. May our experience through your journey show people the light and change their lives.

CONTENTS

My trip home took an hour. I tried everything to distract myself and cheer up. I cranked up the radio and tried to sing my heart out, but that didn't make me feel better. Questions ran through my head. I feared having to say good-bye to Logan way before his time. I quickly pushed such thoughts to the back of my mind. But one question remained—why Logan? How had this become his life? Did people really understand day-to-day life in a cancer world? How could I make people understand this world I'd been forced into kicking and screaming? The questions came quickly. But so did the idea to write this book about pediatric cancer and bring people into this world. I knew I would have to share everything with the readers—my darkest hours, my highest points, my fears, my joys—everything.

But I questioned if I should write this book or even if I could write it. I wondered if I really wanted to relive all the horrible memories. I wondered if I had the strength to share it.

As it turned out, it wasn't about sharing all the horrible things that happened to us; it was about the miracle that happened the day we started using natural remedies. That was the day my son was healed. It wasn't from the chemo, radiation, 3F8, or any other toxic thing. Although that did kill his cancer, it didn't prevent it from coming back. What has prevented it from coming back is all the natural things we started doing and continue to do every day.

This book will detail Logan's journey and everything we did from day one of his diagnosis medically and naturally. I include the journal entries I made on our Caring Bridge blog—a blow-by-blow, almost daily account of Logan's condition so family and friends could follow his progress and send prayers for healing and strength.

This book is a mom telling her story, a mom sharing her worst fear—outliving her child—a mom given renewed hope that miracles do happen and there is a more natural path that is more powerful than you could imagine. Here we go.

Chapter 1

LIFE BEFORE CANCER

A big part of understanding our story is our family situation. My name is Ashleigh, and I married Jason in July 2005. We had Jeffrey Allen on November 22, 2006, and Logan Robert on May 18, 2008. My boys were eighteen months apart, so life was busy, but it seemed perfect.

I took my pregnancies and births as naturally as possible. I watched everything I ate and refused anything unnatural. Even when I suffered from horrible heartburn, I refused to take anything that might affect my babies. I drank milk and ate dry oats at all crazy hours of the night to relieve it. Can you picture a pregnant woman shoving dry oats in her mouth at two in the morning? Well, that was me. Even before they were born, I was protecting them and trying to follow a natural path. I didn't want to risk putting them in harm's way.

My deliveries were natural and drug free. Most woman I know cringe at the idea of going through labor without pain relief. But after attending a birthing class and learning how some pain medicine can pass to the baby, I wanted to try it without these drugs. We hired a doula to attend our birth with Jeffrey. A doula is known as a birth companion. They are a nonmedical person who assists a woman before, during, and after childbirth, by providing physical assistance and emotional support. She was a great help with my breathing and focusing techniques. In the end, I was able to deliver him naturally, with no pain medicine, and it proved to be a beautiful experience. The same was true with Logan and our daughters Hope and Mia, and I wouldn't have it any other way.

I breastfed my children; I wanted to give them the best start possible. Both boys were colicky, so I had to have a very limited diet. So many things would bother their little tummies, so I was very selective about my diet; I cut out dairy and ate only bland foods. It was worth the sacrifice for me. Once I made those changes in my diet, it just became the way, and the kids were much calmer and happier.

Their baby food, juice, and later, table food, were totally organic. I wanted only the best start for them and did everything to make sure they got it in spite of my friends' jokes. At that time, organic was looked upon by most as an unnecessary waste of money.

But there I was, an all-natural mom with a child who ended up with cancer.

Chapter 2

A Tornado Hits Our Happy Home

It was July 2009. Jason and I had spent a year and a half building our dream house. My husband is a builder. When we started dating, I saw plans for a house hanging in his garage. It was his dream house, and it soon became a reality. We worked hard to build our house.

For the first year of Logan's life, I was in essence a single mom. I did the daytime and nighttime routines while Jason worked for his father during the day and worked on our house at night. The boys and I would make quick trips to visit daddy and bring him dinner before the boys would head to bed. It was a sacrifice on both our parts as parents.

The house was done in July. We threw our first huge party for my parents' fortieth wedding anniversary. Life was good!

The next month, Logan developed worrisome symptoms. He started to get fussy and wanted me to hold him pretty much all the time, which wasn't like him. His appetite declined quickly. He grew lethargic. He slept a lot. He ran a low-grade fever off and on for weeks.

One morning, Logan woke up with a huge bruise under his left eye. At first, I thought maybe Jeffrey had hit him or he had bumped into something that I hadn't been aware of. The pictures below showed the bruise starting to appear under his left eye.

I took him to our pediatrician several times that month. At first, they said he wasn't eating because he was cutting his molars, but they couldn't explain the bruise and why it wasn't going away. They never once felt his abdomen for any type of hardness or ordered blood work or a scan.

My third time there, I told our doctor I wanted blood work done. She wrote the prescription but told me it wasn't necessary; she said it could be difficult to draw blood from a baby his age.

As I look back on it, I can't believe I let it go as long as I did. You would think when I told the doctor, "This isn't like my baby. I know something is wrong!" that she would have taken me more seriously and would have listened to the cries of a desperate mother.

I had the prescription for the blood work, but it was a weekend, so the labs were closed. On Saturday night, I tripped going up the stairs in the dark. I hurt my foot and ended up going to the ER first thing Sunday morning. While I was waiting to be seen, Jason took Logan to get his blood work done in the hospital lab. Logan didn't even flinch when they took his blood—not typical behavior for a fifteen-month old; that was another sign something was seriously wrong. Once the blood was drawn, Jason took Logan home to rest because he was looking lethargic. I waited on the doctors.

While I was getting my X-ray, my cell rang. It was someone from our pediatrician's office. She informed me that Logan's blood counts were all off. I was shocked. I was to take Logan immediately to see a hematologist at Lehigh Valley Hospital. I asked her what kind of doctor a hematologist was, and she told me a blood doctor. I wanted to know what could be wrong, and out of her mouth came the word *cancer*.

I don't remember anything after that. I hung up. I wanted to rush the X-rays. Tears were streaming down my face. My foot wasn't broken, but they set me up with a walking cast and crutches. I was sobbing hysterically. I told them to please hurry so I could get to my son. They got me set up quickly, and I called Jason. Another conversation I can't remember—just a blurred message to get Logan to Lehigh Valley Hospital, possible cancer.

I believe now my foot injury was divine intervention. To have hurt it badly enough to go to the hospital got us to the place Logan needed to be. It was as if God had reached down and smacked me in the face, saying, "Go to the hospital now!"

Before I got that call from the pediatrician's office at the hospital, I was upset. I was thinking I'd have to deal with my foot on top of everything else. I kept thinking what awful timing and such horrible luck we'd had. But now I realize it was one of my greatest lessons. Sometimes, we don't understand why something is happening, but in time, we gain perspective. In time, we see and appreciate the timing and the lessons learned. The doctors told us Logan would have died if we had waited even a few more days. So the push to go to the hospital for my foot actually saved my son's life. Timing turned out to be everything!

The first couple of days while Logan was being diagnosed were a horrible blur of tears, breakdowns, and chaos. We finally had an answer to what was wrong with him, but I didn't want to know. I wanted to stay in the dark. I wanted to keep thinking of possibilities like teething, viruses—anything easily treatable. But the blood work demonstrated it was much more serious.

Chapter 3

DETECTING THE DEADLY BEAST

It took a few days before the results came in and the doctors gave us Logan's tentative diagnosis. They suspected it was neuroblastoma, but they wanted to rule out other cancers such as leukemia.

Our first pediatric oncology doctor said he had looked at the cells under the microscope and could see it was not leukemia, and I praised God for that. Though my grandmother had had leukemia and had lived for years with it, I'd lost an aunt to it. I thought of Aunt Susan and her battle and struggle with treatment. I couldn't imagine Logan going through the same treatment she had endured or having the same outcome.

We learned that Logan definitely had neuroblastoma; the cancer had spread. He was stage IV. In the beginning, I refused to let myself google anything on that cancer. Our doctors advised us not to do that, and I'm glad I didn't. It was months if not years before I did.

Neuroblastoma is a rare cancer that almost always affects infants and children; it's the most common type of cancer in infants. There are about 650 cases per year in the United States and 100 cases per year in the UK. Nearly half the cases occur in children younger than two. With neuroblastoma, a solid tumor (a lump or mass caused by uncontrolled or abnormal cell growth) is formed by special nerve cells called neuroblasts. Normally, these immature cells grow and mature into functioning nerve cells, but with neuroblastoma, they become cancer cells. It usually starts in one of the adrenal glands but can also develop in nerve tissues. Neuroblastoma often spreads before any symptoms are apparent, and 50 to 60 percent of neuroblastoma cases spread. That is what was happening to Logan. His original tumor, on his left adrenal gland, had metastasized to a tumor behind his eye.

Neuroblastoma is divided into three risk categories—low, intermediate, and high. Logan was on the worst end of the spectrum; he was at high risk. Neuroblastoma is not well understood; the great majority of cases are sporadic and nonfamilial. Its unknown origins are part of what makes detecting and curing it so difficult.

Now for the really depressing part—the survival statistics. Between 20 and 50 percent of high-risk cases do not respond well to high-dose chemotherapy, and relapse is common. After relapse, the patient is considered "medically incurable." There are some phase I and phase II clinical trials available, but the outcome remains very poor for relapsed, high-risk cases. The majority of those who survive have long-term side effects from treatment. It's estimated that two out of three survivors of childhood cancer will ultimately develop at least one chronic, sometimes life-threatening health problem twenty to forty years after the cancer. So even if you beat the odds and become a survivor, you face future problems. Your worry never really ends. Your fight never seems over.

My in-laws had spoken to our doctor to get some more information after hearing this devastating diagnosis. They'd never heard of neuroblastoma and wanted to know exactly what we were dealing with. Jason and I were still in shock and trying to deal with just the day-to-day drama of having a very sick child. The doctor told them, "Just enjoy every day you have with him." Wow. What a way to go into battle, thinking his days were limited and we should just appreciate what time we had left with him.

Thankfully, Jason and I were not told that at the time; we focused on getting him treatment. It was too hard to focus on the future. According to our doctors, it was a nonexistent future for Logan—not exactly the boost of confidence we needed to hear as we headed into battle.

Chapter 4

Decisions Decisions

We had a diagnosis. We were then faced with what treatment he needed and where we could get that. Our hospital was good, but we wanted a children's hospital and decided to move to CHOP, Children's Hospital of Philadelphia. The doctors there had dealt with many neuroblastoma cases, and of course we felt more confident with them treating our son.

Logan started chemotherapy at CHOP but completed only one round of the national protocol. The national protocol is a standardized treatment plan that detailed the treatment course Logan would complete. Our particular protocol was specific for Logan's diagnosis and stage of cancer. It was a detailed timeline of when chemotherapies, radiation and surgery would occur. While we were at CHOP, we had many signs that just didn't feel right. One example was when the oncologists gave Jason and me a whole list of what we should expect. They listed all the risks associated with using such powerful poisons. Don't get me wrong. Logan was a very sick little boy who needed medical intervention at that point; I don't want you to think I'm saying chemo isn't effective. It can be for some patients, but it isn't what cured my son. It killed his cancer, and we're thankful for that. But it didn't keep his cancer from coming back, which I will get into later.

We went over the huge list of side effects and risks. We signed our son over to their care. The doctor left, and I sobbed at the facts and the realization my son would mostly likely never be able to have children due to the chemo. I sobbed at the damage that could be done to his organs. I sobbed at how sick he would get before he got better. I sobbed at what a long road was ahead of us. Here's an entry I posted on Logan's Caring Bridge site.

CB Entry: Friday, August 28, 2009, 11:08 p.m.

We sat down with the oncologists tonight and had to go over the chemo schedule and side effects of each drug. It has been a very hard evening to say the least. We are trying to not focus on that and just focus on the result of Logan being strong and healthy again.

We thought we would be starting chemo tomorrow, but it looks like it will be Monday, latest Tuesday, until all results are in and we are 100 percent ready to start. While we wait, Logan has still been really lethargic and not feeling well. He did have a few times that he sat up and played and even smiled, and it brought tears to our eyes. Can't wait to see that more often.

CB Entry: Saturday, August 29, 2009, 9:35 p.m.

Today was a good day. My parents, Jason's parents, my sisters, Nick, my niece Alyssa, and Jeffrey all came today to spend some time with Logan and us. They are all staying overnight here in Philly so we will have some more time together tomorrow.

Logan had some Tylenol and a little stronger drug to keep him comfortable today. He got some of his appetite back, and it was so good to see him eat. Never would I have thought I would get so emotional over him taking a bite. Just one of the many small things I am going to start and appreciate through this journey.

Still planning on just resting tomorrow and starting chemo either Monday or Tuesday. He was all swollen/puffy from all the fluids he was getting. Actually gaining 2 pounds in just that fluid weight and now he is back down to his normal skinny self. I missed his chicken legs. I can't be the only one in the family with chicken legs :)

CB Entry: Sunday, August 30, 2009, 7:58 p.m.

Today, Logan got another blood transfusion. His hemoglobin counts went a little low. Once he got that and some meds, he perked up and ate. Watching him play makes all of us tear up.

Family is so important, and it has been wonderful sharing this weekend with everyone. We should be starting chemo tomorrow, so I am extremely nervous but also hopeful to be one day closer to him feeling better.

CB Entry: Monday, August 31, 2009, 8:07 p.m.

They will be starting chemo tomorrow. They were waiting for one test result to come back to be sure on the type of chemo to do. They are sure that it is neuroblastoma, but it could be major or intermediate, which would get different types of treatment. They are leaning toward it being major but want to be sure. We are still praying for intermediate because it would be less chemo and no bone marrow transplant, but we shall see.

CB Entry: Tuesday, September 1, 2009, 6:38 p.m.

They were supposed to start chemo earlier today. While we were waiting to get the results back from pathology, Logan had some issues with his blood counts this morning, so they pushed the chemo back until they figured out what that was.

He had a cat scan today, and they determined the bleeding was most likely from the tumor and they didn't see a ton of fluid/blood in the abdomen. So once the chemo starts to shrink the tumor, the bleeding should stop and his labs should even out.

The report from pathology is that it is a major classification of the neuroblastoma, which is what they expected, so they know for sure the course of chemo to do. The chemo is on order, and he is all prepped with fluids so they should be starting it within the hour.

I am *so* nervous to see how the night goes with that but anxious for it to start. He has been in so much pain these last couple days that he needs something. Please continue to pray for him.

After signing off on all the chemo orders, my best childhood friend Laura came to see us on her way home from work. I sat with her and cried. I told her everything they said about the side effects, and she tried her best to keep my spirits up. She said, "They don't know Logan. They don't know how strong he is. He is going to beat this, Ash."

As we were talking, one of the doctors walked in to give me a copy of all the side effects she had gone over with us. She had pranced in complaining about how crappy the weather was outside and how she was not looking forward to being out in it. She didn't even seem fazed by the news she had just delivered or the fact I had a box of nearly empty tissues on my lap and eyes completely soaked and swollen. Oh, I'm sorry. My son is lying in a hospital bed and at death's door. You just read me all the negative side effects I could see my son go through just so he doesn't die and you're complaining about how dreary it is outside? Really? She expressed no sympathy, compassion—nothing; she was just a doctor delivering information and checking off the last thing she had to do before heading home to her healthy family. That was one sign we were not in the right place. How could I have a doctor who had absolutely no compassion for a mother and her son? How could I put my trust in her that she would be sympathetic on this long road? It didn't sit well with me.

When Logan was getting his initial scans at CHOP, we received yet another indicator we might have been at the wrong hospital. Logan's cheeks appeared swollen. They ordered another scan of his face because that hadn't been included in the original workup. We were upset Logan would need to be sedated again and subject to more radiation. We knew we just needed to start chemo and didn't feel it was necessary to do that. So we declined the further testing and just said we wanted to start treatment.

We had apparently annoyed the doctor. As I was walking down the hall, I passed his oncologist, the woman who had delivered the fabulous side-effect news with such grace and joy. She refused to make eye contact with me and completely ignored me as we passed in the narrow hallway. I felt like a high school sophomore passing a senior who considered me beneath her.

I ignored her rudeness and focused on getting treatment started to give Logan a chance of feeling better. Once we started the first round of chemo, the swelling in his cheek disappeared instantly. Shock! We were thankful for saving our son undue testing and unnecessary radiation. In the below pictures, you can see the bruising under the eye and swollenness in the cheek.

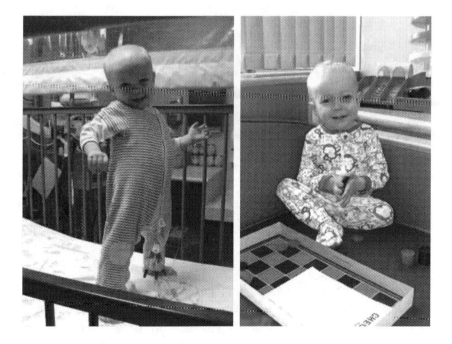

We quickly became Logan's biggest advocates; we made sure each scan, test, and procedure made sense to us, and we spared him the danger of too much radiation. We maintained that attitude throughout his whole health journey. We realized the importance of protecting his long-term health prospects as much as we could while still active in their treatment plan. We tried to go with our guts as his parents; we knew only we were truly there for Logan. He was not just another patient with an ID number. He was our baby. He was our life.

The final realization that we were not where we needed to be was when I was on the phone with another oncologist from CHOP. We had finished a round of chemo, and we were asking questions. We wanted to know statistics, something any parent would want to know in that situation. It was a learning process for us. As we asked our questions, I felt I was bothering him. He sounded almost annoyed that we were asking such questions. The final straw was when I asked the doctor why they were doing all this if there was such a terribly low survival rate. Why put these children through such horrible treatments if they really don't think it will work? He said, "Everything we do is for all the future Logans of the world." It was for research. Not my Logan but for future children. They would document and research all their findings on Logan so they could help kids in the future who developed neuroblastoma. At that point, I was done. I realized then that all their efforts weren't for my son but for more information, research. I realized we were in the wrong hospital.

We were very fortunate that once we did start chemo, Logan was very responsive to it. It made him feel better. His cancer cells were very sensitive to the chemo and luckily died off quickly. He actually perked up and was smiling again. The tumors began to shrink. The huge bruising under his eye started to lighten, so we knew it was working. We were very excited to see the progress with Logan in such a short time. He went from lying down and being totally unresponsive to actually being up, playing and laughing within days of starting chemo. It was a huge change in such a short period. It really gave us hope that things were going to be okay. Below is a picture right after the first round of chemo; it shows his beautiful smile we hadn't seen in a long time. Amazing!

We felt he wasn't that close to death's door. We felt we could breathe a second and focus on other places for treatment. That's exactly what we did.

When he was first diagnosed, my sister, Celeste, had done some research and found Memorial Sloan Kettering Cancer Center (MSKCC) in New York, a leader in neuroblastoma treatment. She had given me information on their new therapies and 3F8. All those words were foreign to me at the time, but just then, I began to think of them as an option.

We immediately did a conference call with one of Sloan's neuroblastoma oncologists. He had nothing but nice things to say about CHOP and concurred that they followed the same national protocol up until the end.

Although the first several rounds of chemo on the protocol were the same, Sloan did not do bone marrow transplants. The doctors there felt that the bone marrow transplant required by the national protocol didn't result in higher rates of survival. At that time, CHOP was doing a random study. Half the children in the study had one transplant, and the other half had two. Based on the results, they would decide what their protocol would be for all children. We didn't take the bone marrow transplant lightly. It is basically like taking your child to death's door and trying to recover him or her. We were really against the thought that our son might be randomly chosen to endure two for research purposes. We believed Sloan's findings concerning survival and relapse rates.

It seemed to us that Sloan treated each child more individually. Jason and I talked for days about this, and we just knew we had to move Logan there, and we did. It just felt right. CHOP is a great hospital, and I'm sure there are insensitive doctors at all hospitals. We moved because we liked the idea of having a team of neuroblastoma experts who would avoid putting Logan through a bone marrow transplant. Sloan is also known to be on the cutting edge of research and therapies. So moving hospitals was the right choice for us.

MSKCC always made us feel there was hope and promise. They always looked at Logan with positivity and sometimes even rose-colored glasses, and we needed that. They gave us the same information as other hospitals had but made us feel that each child handles treatment differently and we should have hope. Miracles do happen.

We continued with the protocol at MSKCC. After four rounds of chemo, they performed surgery on Logan to remove the tumor in his abdomen. We were thrilled that his surgeon was world-renowned in the field of neuroblastoma.

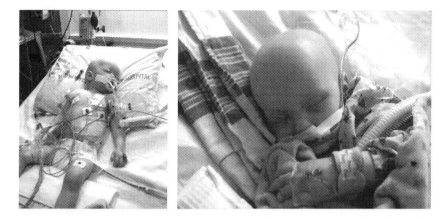

The pictures above were in the PICU in New York immediately following Logan's tumor removal. Logan basically lay in bed on a ventilator and was sedated for about a week. Nothing could have prepared us for that. I didn't know if I could get through the deep stress Jason and I were under. Yes, we were thrilled the surgery had been a success. Yes, we were happy to hear the tumor was dead. But no, we weren't prepared for the days and days of watching him just lie there almost lifeless. The only signs of life were the numbers on the machines. We knew his body needed time to heal; we knew he needed rest. But it was nevertheless the worst image to see day after day. I wanted to see him smile. I wanted to see his beautiful blue eyes. He was tied to that bed and hooked up to monitors, so there was no way for me to hold my sweet child and comfort him.

So far in this journey, Logan was attached to my hip. All he wanted to do those days was lie on me and snuggle with his special blue blanket. Holding him gave him comfort, but it also gave me comfort. It made me feel I was giving him peace and security, and he gave that back to me. At that time in his hospital room, I felt numb, alone. I wasn't able to do what felt natural, what I needed to do—hold my baby. That was something I'd never experienced before or ever want to again.

Caring Bridge is the blog on which we posted updates on Logan. Each entry detailed that day's ordeals and happenings. It helped me get through the difficult times. The writing was a sort of therapy for me, and the prayers we received lifted us up to carry us through.

CB Entry: December 2, 2009, 9:26 a.m.

We met with our surgeon, Dr. Laquaglia, yesterday. He is one of if not the best surgeons for neuroblastoma in the world and one of the main reasons we moved Logan to Sloan. It was good to finally meet him but also very scary to think of all that could happen.

Dr. Laquaglia went over in detail Logan's CT scan. He told us Logan's tumor had originated from his left adrenal gland. So they will be taking that out along with the tumor. His right adrenal gland looks fine, so that will just pick up the work of the missing left one, and he should be fine that way. There is also a possibility that they would have to take Logan's left kidney if there was too much damage done to the artery that goes to the kidney. He won't know that until he is in there, but that is really rare. It has only happened about 18 times in the last 25 years of him doing them, but he has to give us all the worst-case scenarios.

I believe he said he does about 150 of these surgeries a year. We are to be at Sloan by 7 on Monday, and surgery is scheduled for 9. They told us it will be a long day. Surgery can take anywhere from 4 to 6 hours—sometimes less, sometimes longer.

After surgery, they will be taking Logan right across the street to the PICU at that hospital. Sloan has an ICU but not a pediatric one, so he will stay there for 2–3 days before going back to Sloan inpatient for round five of chemo. We will stay inpatient for that round so they can keep monitoring him.

Dr. Laquaglia did comment a few times on how cute Logan was, and of course we could not argue that. We told him to make sure he got his rest this weekend to be ready for Monday, and of course he thought that was funny.

We also got all the blood work necessary to check all his counts. Both his lines from his temporary port worked great. They will be putting in a new line. This one will be under his skin with no tubes hanging. Good thing is Logan will be able to get in the tub with Jeffrey and even swim. Hopefully, it won't be a pain to access. Because he is so small, it is hard to explain what we are doing, so we have to hold them down. We are just praying that process goes as smoothly as everything else has been going.

Just enjoying this week at home with my boys. Please pray that Logan will do amazing on Monday as I know he will. It is going to be a long next 2 weeks for us, but we are ready to take it on. And keeping in mind we will be home for Christmas gives us something else to look forward to.

CB Entry: December 5, 2009, 1:34 p.m.

So Monday is the *big* day. Of course, it has been on our minds all week and weekend. We have been getting some great advice as to what to expect as to prepare ourselves. Thanks, Danielle!

The hardest thing is going to have to see Logan all tubed up and out of it. We are getting used to seeing our little

20

boy all energetic and happy, so it is going to be very hard emotionally to deal with that again. But we know it is necessary and just one step closer to remission.

We are planning on staying at the Ronald McDonald House tomorrow night. They want us there at 7 in the morning and surgery is scheduled for 9. They want us there in case the first appointment, which is usually an easy and quick procedure, might be canceled or done early and then we are up.

Please pray that Logan will handle the surgery amazing, as we know he will and that we won't be in the PICU long at Cornell. We hope our stay there is short so that we can be back at Sloan and receive the fifth and hopefully last round of chemo. Pray that Jason and I will have enough strength to help Logan through this and stay strong. Also pray for Jeffrey that he understands why we are away and will just enjoy his time with his Grandma, Pop-pop, Mimi, and Pappy.

CB Entry: December 7, 2009, 1:12 p.m.

So today is the big surgery day. We were here at Sloan by 7:00 a.m.—well, 6:30 actually, because who could sleep? Not us. Unfortunately, the first procedure scheduled before Logan took longer than they thought, so instead of starting at 9, it was 11:30 before they sedated him and took him back.

What an amazing little trooper he is. He hasn't eaten or drank anything since bedtime last night, and he was so smiley this morning. He would motion that he wanted to eat, but we would just distract him. He also took a good nap on Jason, so that took up a bunch of the waiting time. Pappy and Mimi were here first thing this morning and got some good visiting time in. Mimi even was also able to do reiki, which is always good.

They called us 1:30 and said the double lumen mediport was in and they were about to do the incision to open him up. When they were prepping us, they said it would be 2 hours of prep time/inserting tubes/the line all before they would even open him up. We should be going over soon to take a tour of the PICU. It will help to pass the time. They give updates every two hours, and we just pray that God is working overtime this morning :) We had a very encouraging meeting with the surgeon before he went in and know we are at the best place. We will send more updates as we know.

CB Entry: December 7, 2009, 7:20 p.m.

Lots to report. The surgery went really well! Dr. Laquaglia said the tumor looked dead, praise God! Now they will of course have to send it to pathology for testing, but it is very promising that after all his experience that he would say it looked dead. He said that means the chemo is working great. He only lost about 50 to 100 ccs of blood during surgery, so that was good.

The mediport is in on the right side, and they will take the temporary port out once we are back at Sloan. He has an epidural for pain management tomorrow. He doesn't need it now since he is sedated, but tomorrow, it will be great for pain management.

The artery to the kidney looked good. They did end up taking his left adrenal gland out since that is where the tumor was, but he should have no side effects since the right one looks good and has been doing the work for both all these months. Seventy-five percent of these tumors come from the adrenal gland—fun little fact for you.

Dr. Laquaglia did have one little surprise when he got in there. Logan had what is called Meckel's diverticulum. You can check out this link to get the full read on it because of course you know that was the first place I went. Basically, it is an appendix off the small bowel. It occurs in about 2 percent of the population, so of course my little man had to be signed up for that. Usually, the tissue is smooth but Logan's was a little funny looking, so he just took it out so not to worry about it or cause problems later. It can cause ulcers and bleeding when kids are older, so now we don't have to worry about it. Another reason to have such a wonderful and experienced surgeon to make judgment calls like that to save Logan pain or problems in the future.

After we talked to Dr. Laquaglia, we waited some more until they were ready to transport Logan to the PICU. We were prepared as much as parents and grandparents can be to how he would look—super puffy and all tubed up but resting comfortably. It took them some more time to get him settled here before we were allowed in. Then Logan had a little issue with his breathing. They checked the machine because as new patients come in, they have to work with the settings to make sure it is at a right pace for Logan's weight. They did a quick EKG to check his heart, which looks fine. They will be constantly checking his blood/gas levels to make sure he is getting enough oxygen.

23

Even though the day has been long, we appreciated sharing it with Logan's Mimi and Pappy. Seeing Logan like this is so hard and very emotional, but we are staying strong and excited to have this huge hurdle over with. I know it is going to be a long night, but I know God is watching over and will protect Logan. Please say a prayer that Logan does well tonight, and we will be back at Sloan as soon as he is ready.

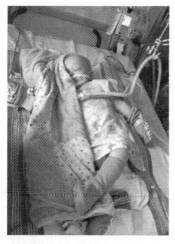

CB Entry: December 8, 2009, 7:42 a.m.

Logan did great last night. He was comfortable and sleeping all night. For me, sleeping—or should I say attempting to sleep—in the PICU was interesting to say the least. Now I know why they sedate the babies because there is no way they would sleep otherwise. As for the moms, that isn't the case. It is constant beeping and checking, but even though it was a long night for me, Logan is comfortable, and that is what is important.

We are sharing this room with 2 other patients, so we are anxious to go back to Sloan, where we have a private room and a whole lot less noise. He was on 25 with the ventilator last night and is down to 18, so they think he is breathing mostly on his own and will take that tube out today. Hurray! One less tube to worry about, and when he wakes up, it won't be irritating.

He did start pulling at it last night while in and out of sleep, so they had to restrain his arms, but they also gave him more medicine, so he was in a deeper sleep and more comfortable. I know that sounds harsh to restrain his arms, but he has a lot of important tubes in, and even though he is sleeping, sometimes, he flares his arms, and it is important he doesn't pull out or move any of them until the doctors feel they are ready to come out. He really has no idea what is going on right now and is just resting.

Praying the breathing tube comes out today and that Logan wakes up. It is good to see him resting because I know he isn't in pain, but mommy misses his big blue eyes and beautiful smile. Will keep you updated as the day progresses.

CB Entry: December 8, 2009, 1:13 p.m.

It looks like they will not be taking the breathing tube out today. After the doctors saw him in their rounds, they said he was puffier then they expected and would rather let him rest today. So they want to keep it in to help his breathing so it isn't labored. His blood pressure was a little low, so they are closely monitoring him.

They did another X-ray and saw he has a little fluid in his lungs, so they are holding off on the fluids and putting him on a different ventilator. It is like the one he is on, but this one actually shoots pressure into the lungs so it helps push past the fluid and open them all the way up. For as much fluid as he has gotten, he hasn't been peeing a whole lot, so they are going to just watch him and wait for his body to release the fluid.

He has been sleeping today due to the sedation, but it is best to keep him calm and resting so he can heal. Please pray that Logan will start to release the fluid on his own to help with the puffiness and that his blood pressure and heart rate stay will at a good rate so that they can take the tube out and we can go to Sloan.

CB Entry: December 9, 2009, 9:08 a.m.

Logan had a good night. He slept great and only had one time that they had a hard time settling him. They even gave him back-to-back doses of fentanyl, and he was still moving around. After a little coaxing with his blankey, he finally settled. The nurse asked me how his personality was because he seems like a fighter. I just laughed and told her she has no idea.

Last night, they wanted to put a small catheter in Logan's right side of his chest. His left side already has a drain in from surgery, and an X-ray showed there was a little fluid outside his lung. This is normal since they are giving him so much fluid and he wasn't peeing much of it out.

Jason and I felt a little uncomfortable doing that. There are risks with puncturing the lung, and we wanted to see if Logan could get rid of it himself. When he had this puffy issue before, the Lasix worked great to get it off. They were waiting on giving the Lasix until his blood pressure stayed level since earlier in the day it was low. So we asked the doctors if it would be okay to just wait and see if Logan's body would get rid of the once he had the Lasix.

Finally around 6, they gave him Lasix. His blood pressure did go down a bit, so they gave him blood pressure medicine to bring it up. Right now it seems like a balancing act, and it can be frustrating. With surgery, it throws off all Logan's fluid levels, and they have to wait until they level out, but in the meantime, they have to watch and control any levels that get too low or too high. The blood-pressure medicine dopamine worked great, and everything was stable again. The Lasix of course did work, and through the night he peed a lot.

We met with the doctors this morning, and they wanted to keep him sedated and the tube in until more fluid comes off. They might take the tube out later today or tomorrow morning. If his blood pressure stays good, they will increase the Lasix, which will just help him get rid of the fluid.

We had in our minds to be back at Sloan by now, but we know that this sedation/resting time is really doing Logan good after the surgery. We feel comfortable with the doctors here and think it is best to give Logan time to release the fluid before we do anything.

Our surgeon, Dr. Laquaglia, stopped in last night to check on Logan. He said that his swollenness looked fine and this was all normal after surgery. He said he thinks he looks good. We told him about the fluid in the chest, and he agreed the Lasix should take care of it and if not, the catheter is no big deal. We gave him one of our Christmas cards with Logan and Jeffrey's pictures, and he said he would hang it in the clinic. I told him he could totally put it on his desk framed, that would be fine. He laughed and said, "Oh, so, you both are comedians." It was a good laugh and nice to see him.

Please pray that Logan will lose this extra fluid and not be as swollen and that the tube will be taken out smoothly. Although we are anxious to get back to Sloan to start treatment, we are happy Logan is getting this time to rest and heal from surgery. I think God is taking a hand in this to make sure Logan gets enough time before we start round five.

CB Entry: December 10, 2009, 8:04 a.m.

Logan had a very restful night last night. The doctors just made their rounds. They looked at Logan's X-ray that was taken this morning and saw there was much less fluid near the lung, so the Lasix did work. The plan is that they are going to start taking him off sedation this morning, and when he wakes up, they will take the breathing tube out. Meanwhile, they will be starting his epidural, which will help with his abdominal pain control when he wakes up. With the epidural, he will be able to sit up and move around, and we just will have to be careful so that he doesn't pull it out since it isn't stitched in.

We should get the pathology report from the tumor in about a week from surgery day, so we are hoping to get that tomorrow. Praying that the tumor was all dead tissue as Dr. Laquaglia suspected so that perhaps our course of treatment will be less and we can start immunotherapy sooner.

Please pray for Logan to wake up with as little as pain as possible considering everything he has been through. Also pray that he is in remission. Will keep everyone updated on how he does when he wakes up.

CB Entry: December 10, 2009, 4:48 p.m.

So they did a test today for 20 mins to see if Logan could breathe on his own. He did great and was able to, but they still turned the machine back on. Until he wakes all the way up, they can't take the tube out. If they take the tube out and he immediately falls asleep, he might have trouble breathing and they would have to put the tube back in. No fun. So we have to make sure he wakes on his own and stays a wake for a while.

His blood pressure and heart rate have all been good today. He was on dopamine, but they took him off that, and he continues to maintain great blood pressure. He is still on the Lasix drip, so his urine output has been good, which is allowing him to start looking more like little Logan. I am starting to see his little chicken legs a bit, and mommy missed them.

Praying Logan wakes up on his own soon so that tube can come out and that he has another restful night. We probably won't be back at Sloan until late tomorrow, more likely Saturday. Jason is planning on going to Sloan tomorrow and talk with Dr. Kushner. Just to give us maybe a tentative game plan on what they are thinking will happen, and to see if the pathology report is back in.

Please pray that the pathology report confirms the tumor was all dead tissue and that Logan will wake happy, rested, and comfortable.

CB Entry: December 11, 2009, 10:42 a.m.

They ended up never taking the breathing tube out. Logan's oxygen level went down last night. They aren't sure why since all his numbers were great yesterday, and his X-ray this morning looked even better then yesterday. So the doctors are confused as to why his blood pressure and everything looks good but this one number isn't as high as it should be. It is around 92 and should be around 100.

So they retaped his tube thinking it is a mechanical problem and took another X-ray. Now we just wait and watch for that number to come back up. They had to sedate him again to keep him comfortable and until they can figure out why it went down. The doctor said it is frustrating because it makes no sense and he looks great, but it's only a bump in the road. They did turn the air pressure up on the ventilator and said that could have happened if there are some folds in the lungs that didn't all the way expand out; it could cause that so the huge breaths the machine simulates would take care of that.

Please pray that Logan's oxygen level will come back up and we will be able to take the tube out. We have seen him open his eyes a few times, and it is such a tease. We can't wait for him to be back to his normal self.

CB Entry: December 11, 2009, 2:03 p.m.

I can't even type right now. The pathology came back in and the tumor was all dead! Yea! Dr. Kushner is coming over later to talk to us. When we first talked about it being all dead, they said it was so rare; in only 2 out of a hundred kids (2 percent) are the tumors found to be all dead. Maybe now the doctors will look at Logan like the little amazing angel we all know he is.

Logan is still having trouble with his oxygen numbers, but they aren't too bad, and we are just watching them. Pray that goes up so we can take the tube out. I just *so* needed that news today.

CB Entry: December 12, 2009, 11:58 a.m.

Logan's numbers are great. Overnight, his oxygen went up to 100 percent, where it has stayed. He is on 40 with the ventilator and a pressure (PEEP) of 7, which needs to be a 5 when he is extubated. He is also at a 12 setting for SIMV, which is the amount of breaths it simulates a minute.

The doctors just made their rounds and the plan for today is they decreased the PEEP number to 6 and the SIMV to 10 and will see how he does with that. If he holds his oxygen, they will decrease it even more later today. They are planning on extubating him tomorrow morning. They will take him off the Midazolam drop probably around 4 in the morning so that he will hopefully be awake by 6 to take the tube out. Our problem before was that even though they took him off the sedation, he slept a full 24 hours. So we need to make sure he wakes up and is alert enough to take it out.

Had a wonderful visit with Mimi and Pappy yesterday. Jason and I even got out to celebrate Logan's good news about the tumor to a nice Italian New York dinner— thanks, Mimi and Pappy. Dr. Kushner never got to make it over last night, so we are anxious to talk to him once we return to Sloan and get the game plan.

We are visiting with Brandy and Nick today. It is so good to see his oxygen at 100 percent. We pray that his counts will continue to hold so he can be extubated tomorrow!

CB Entry: December 13, 2009, 8:38 a.m.

Logan is breathing *totally* on his own. He did great overnight, and they pulled the tube out early this morning. They put him on a little oxygen through a face mask and then a nose tube, but he wasn't on it long and is doing great on his own. When he first woke up, he was a little uncomfortable. His throat is going to be a little sore for a while since that tube was in there so long and irritating it. So our nurse gave him a little morphine, and he has been comfortable ever since. He has been looking all around and just taking it all in. He is sleeping now.

We are waiting for the doctors to do their rounds before we know what the next step is. The surgeon team should be stopping by today to check Logan's other tubes. He has a tube coming from his abdomen that has been draining fluid from the surgery site. There has been no real fluid collection in the last 2 days, so that is a sign it is ready to come out. He also has a tube running from his nose to his stomach, which they also feel is ready to come out. That is the surgeon's call, so hopefully, that team will be by and we can get those out today. Will update more when we hear from the team.

Please pray that Logan will remain fully oxygenated today on his own and that he is comfortable. We are expecting a visit from Celeste and Rob today and are looking forward to it.

As soon as he was finally off the ventilator, I climbed into bed with him. We still didn't move him because we didn't want him agitated, but I got as close as I could. It felt amazing. I felt we were reunited.

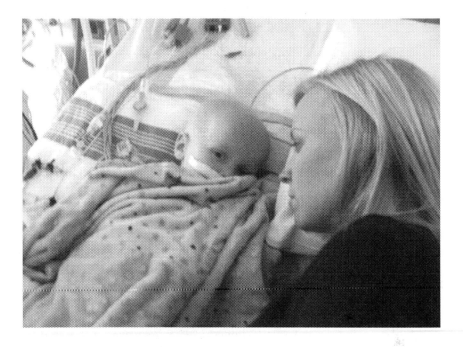

When they removed the tumor and had it tested, the cells were completely dead, which was a *huge* blessing. The chemo had been very effective in killing the cancer cells. However, they continued with round five of chemo, the hardest round ever, while his fragile body was still trying to recuperate from surgery. Below is a picture of him not at the PICU but at Sloan inpatient getting the fifth round of chemo. Logan's expression says it all. He just felt awful and held tightly to his special blue blanket.

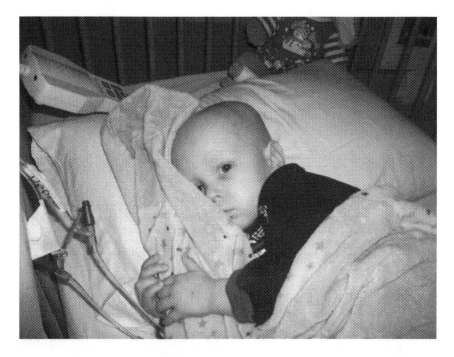

It was right before Christmas when we brought Logan home to heal and rest. We thought how wonderful it would be to be home for Christmas. Any place is better than the hospital on any day but especially on holidays. Unfortunately, Logan was *so* sick that it was really hard to enjoy. He just lay around, barely strong enough to hold his head up. His body needed time to heal from the surgery and to recover his counts from that last round of chemo. He barely ate and he couldn't talk or smile or join his brother in opening presents. It was a very emotional Christmas for the whole family. Seeing Logan like that was heartbreaking. It hurt us all and is a horrible memory. Even the days after Christmas were spent in the hospital dealing with issues instead of being home organizing all the toys and Christmas mess, which most people just take for granted.

These following pictures always make me cry. Even Santa couldn't elicit a tiny smile from his pain-racked face. It just makes my heart hurt to think of how badly he felt at such a blessed time.

CB Entry: December 25, 2009, 7:50 p.m.

Merry Christmas to everyone! We were happy to not be in the hospital at this time and enjoyed the day with my family. Logan was still really out of sorts and still not eating or drinking a lot. He had a few bites of applesauce and some sips of juice but not enough. It was a hard day for my family and us to see Logan like this. We all miss his smile and "scoot."

Please pray tonight that Logan will wake up tomorrow and start to eat and drink as he used too. We are several days out from chemo and are just waiting for him to turn the corner. If he doesn't pick up tomorrow, we are considering not waiting until Monday for his appointment and taking him in for a check. We totally do not want to do that or the possibility of a feeding tube, but it might be our only option. The power of prayer has done so much so far, so please focus your prayers that Logan will start to eat as he used to and get his energy and weight back.

CB Entry: December 26, 2009, 7:08 p.m.

So I ended up bringing Logan to Lehigh Valley Hospital since he wasn't drinking as much as he should and his appetite was still not good. I was more worried about the drinking, though, for the possibility of dehydration. Jason called the on-call doctor at Sloan, who said he should be drinking 20 ounces a day, and I knew he hasn't been drinking near that. So I came down here around 1.

They put him on fluids and took his blood to check all his counts and electrolytes. His fluid level was low, but he was not dehydrated. They put him on fluids and figured they would just watch him overnight.

He did perk up a bit and was smiling for me, which was good to see. He ate some bread and a whole container of applesauce, which he ended up throwing up. Thought we were out of the woods with that, but it must have just been too much at once since he really hasn't eaten much. They gave him some Zofran for that, and he went to sleep and is resting now. They also gave him his Neupogen shot since his ANC is down to 80. They were expecting us to go home tomorrow morning, but it really depends on if he starts to drink on his own. Please pray that he does eat and drink and that his stomach calms. They did weigh him and he is around 18 pounds, so we need to get that weight up.

CB Entry: December 27, 2009, 7:27 p.m.

We are *home!* We met with our doctor from the Lehigh Valley Clinic, and he said that Logan would need platelets (which we got this afternoon) and then we could go home and just set up for a homecare nurse to come tomorrow. She will be setting us up with a fluid bag for Logan to get hydrated at night, and then he would be unhooked from it during the day to drink as he pleases.

If he happens to drink enough tomorrow, we won't have to do that, so that is one of our prayers tonight. Logan did throw up his lunch again today, and the doctors told me that even if he wants more, I have to limit his intake to only a few bites and then wait a full hour before giving him more. Today, I waited 15 mins. or so in between several bites, but it wasn't enough. So once we got home, I was giving him some applesauce, but he was pointing to the brown rice and beef stroganoff my mom had made. So I gave him a few bites of that, and he thoroughly enjoyed it. Even though he wanted more, I waited an hour before giving him some more. It all stayed down—*phew!*

Before bed, he had a couple of animal crackers, which is also a good sign of him eating more types of things. Praying he has a restful night and hopefully continues to slowly get back into the routine of eating and drinking.

Chapter 5

3F8—Pain Therapy

Once he completed chemotherapy, we rejoiced. He had done it! What seemed like a long road ended up almost flying because of his strict chemo schedule. For those couple of months, the schedule was the same and pretty predictable. They would give Logan a round of chemo, watch his counts fall, watch his counts rise, and then hit him again with another round all in a matter of weeks. A tedious and scary process became almost routine. We didn't even focus on the long-term side effects anymore but just marked each round down, knowing he was one step closer to being done and reaching remission.

Now that chemo was over and he got the all-clear scans, Logan was considered to be in *remission*— a beautiful state, a place we were so very thankful to have reached. It was painful to see many children along the way still struggling and not having the same response to treatment. Some relapsed quickly and had to begin treatments again. Some died before Logan had completed his protocol, which was devastating. Meeting these beautiful souls, sharing stories with their parents, and watching them earn their angel wings *way* before their time was heartrending. It is a part of Logan's journey I live with and think about every day. It has changed me as a person. It has changed me as a mom.

Although we were basking in the light of remission, we weren't done. Now that they had rid Logan's body of cancer cells, they wanted to try to keep the cancer away. Our next process involved 3F8, an antibody treatment Sloan Kettering offers. Very simply, antibody treatment is injecting the body with medicine that is supposed to teach the body to recognize and fight neuroblastoma cells if they present themselves. For some reason, Logan's body didn't recognize these cells as bad or immature, and his body didn't attack the cells, and that allowed them to multiply and form a tumor. The 3F8 treatment is supposed to train the body to do that, so they wanted him to complete as many rounds as possible to get in as much of this mouse antibody they could. They complete rounds as long as the children tolerate it and their bodies don't reach HAMA. HAMA positive is detected by blood work and basically means the body has accepted the mouse antibody and the 3F8 is no longer effective.

The 3F8 is an awful process to say the least. While the antibody is being infused, the patients feel intense pain. Since neuroblastoma has to do with the nerves, the antibodies go to the nerve endings and make the body feel that it is being attacked, and extreme pain is the result. So basically, the child screams, cries, and begs you to please stop it and help him. It was the most grueling sound and most draining week of my life. Each day, these little warriors climb up into those beds to be hooked up to the machines, knowing they will cause pain *all* with the hopes that it will keep the cancer away. During the infusion, their breathing becomes erratic and their heart rates can reach into the 200s. It is extremely taxing on the body. Even with the high doses of pain medicine, they still feel intense pain.

I was fortunate that Logan was so young when he started, and I hoped he would never remember it. But I do think that such a traumatic experience will be locked away in his brain forever. Children do have just the most amazing strength and resilience; they can go from a painful treatment, rest for a few hours, and be up and playing later that day. Little miracles is the best way to describe them. I spent so much time in awe of what Logan took on. He dealt with each situation with such strength that I actually drew strength from him. "Some people have never met their heros. I gave birth to mine." How very true for oncology mothers.

Here are some of the CB journal entries from our first week of 3F8. I was more informative and trying to stay positive on Caring

Bridge. No matter how hard the day was, I would give the information and try to focus on the positives. It helped me get through the week but didn't really paint an honest picture of what was going on.

The beginning rounds of 3F8 were a bit easier than the later rounds. As he got older and more vocal, his cries, "*Ouch*, Mommy! Please stop that. Please stop!" made the process much harder on both of us and will forever haunt me.

CB Entry: February 14, 2010, 8:37 p.m.

Tomorrow, we will be heading to Sloan to start the 3F8. We are to be in clinic by 8 and should be starting soon after. *Please* keep us in your prayers all week and especially tomorrow, as none of us knows what to expect. I just pray Logan handles this treatment as he has all the others, with strength and amazement.

Had a *wonderful* weekend with family. We were finally able to get some of the cousins together, which they all enjoyed. Logan had some special moments with his Auntie KK; he walked to her and reached for her. And Elizabeth remarked how good Logan looks and doesn't look sick anymore. It really warmed us all to see the interaction and pure love for one another.

Praying for God to be with us tomorrow as I know he will be.

CB Entry: February 15, 2010, 3:20 p.m.

Day one of 3F8 is over, *phew!* They weren't able to start the infusion until 1:30. Monday mornings are always crazy here, and it takes forever to get the meds from the pharmacy. Luckily, Tuesdays thru Fridays go much quicker (at least that is what they say) since the orders are put in the night before. So hopefully tomorrow, we should be able to start by 8 or 9 in the morning and not have it be such a long day.

A dance therapist came in right before we started. She was great. She works with the younger 3F8 patients and had such a calming presence about her. She played with Logan with some instruments, colorful scarfs, and his favorite item of all—bubbles. She showed us techniques on how to rock with him almost in a meditative state.

About 8 minutes or so into the infusion, Logan started to tense up. And it was basically pure pain for about 15 min. He did amazingly, though, and the nurses said he did really great. His breathing was good through the whole thing, which is what they worry about since some kids hold their breath during it. They said the first day is the worst; it does get better.

When they started the infusion, they gave him no pain meds. With the younger kids, they don't want to overmedicate them since all kids deal with the pain differently. So once it started, they gave him a quarter-dose of a pain med Dilaudid. Then a little later, they gave him some Benadryl, since he got really red. Then they ended up giving him one more quarter-dose of Dilaudid. Then he fell fast asleep and has been resting comfortably ever since. He woke up a couple of times to drink but went back to sleep, so we are letting him rest.

We will head back to the Ronald McDonald House tonight and be back in the clinic by 8. Hoping tomorrow won't be as long as a day. Please pray that this process will just get easier and easier for Logan. We know God was watching over us, and I feel like he sent that dance therapist *just* for us ☺

CB Entry: February 16, 2010, 11:04 a.m.

Logan did really well last night. He was a little fussy when we got back to the Ronald House and didn't want dinner. So we gave him some pain meds, and he fell asleep around 6. He slept straight through the night until 6 this morning. He woke up happy and ate breakfast for us.

Today went *so* much better. Logan did *great!* They started the infusion at 11:30 this morning. This time, they did give him a half-dose of pain meds before starting and another half-dose in the middle of the infusion. He had a great time chewing and playing with the breathing tube (as you can see by the picture attached).

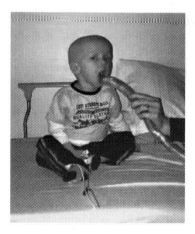

We had another dance therapist come in during the infusion. Logan cried out only a few times before settling. I think I have the rocking and "swooshing" thing down. The dance therapist said Logan and I were very in tune with each, and she thinks that is why he does so well. I agree!

The nurses were also so happy with how he did. They said this is just great and are surprised at how well he handled it. The one nurse actually said, "Logan seemed to just know and accept it and just go with it."

We also met with Dr. Cheung, the creator of 3F8. He is an extremely brilliant man, and it was a pleasure talking to him. He answered some of our questions, and we feel very comfortable with this path.

He is resting comfortably now. Please pray that tomorrow, the infusion will go even better and we will be home before we know it. Please always pray that the reason for these treatments, *to keep him in remission,* will work.

Even while doing such a traumatic medical treatment, I know the dance therapist really helped Logan. She came into the room before the infusion started and the mesmerization or distraction began. Logan was able to begin focusing on something other than the pain that was about to come. She reminded me a lot of the doula I used during childbirth. The dance therapists played special music, used scarves as distractions, and even played games like balancing toys on his head, all in the hopes to keep his mind occupied. The pain gets to a point that nothing helps. However, I feel all those techniques we did helped Logan get through the worst of it.

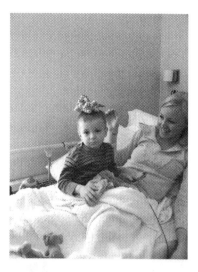

Chapter 6

THE BEAST RETURNS

He had just completed the fourth round of 3F8 and was home resting. His normal, three-month scans were set up for the following week. Logan started acting as if something was bothering him. He would rub his head once in a while and just not act happy and normal. I commented to Jason, "I just don't get it. He's on no medication right now. What could be bothering him?"

The next day, he spiked a fever, and we went to our local hospital. They drew blood cultures and were about to discharge him. Since he wasn't neutropenic (blood counts bottomed out), we were allowed to go home. As they were giving us our discharge papers, Logan, who was lying on me, started to tense up and make a weird motion with his lips. It took us a couple of seconds to realize what was happening. He was having a seizure. It was one of the most helpless and horrifying moments. We sat by and watched as doctors struggled to stabilize him and put in a breathing tube. He lay on the table with his eyes rolled back in his head, just slightly jerking from the seizure. My heart slowed to the point I felt like it was going to stop. We had no idea what had caused the seizure. Maybe a febrile seizure due to his high fever? He was quickly moved to the PICU, and an MRI revealed our worst fears. Logan had a brain tumor. It was exactly nine months since he had been diagnosed. I have to say the first relapse almost hit us harder than the actual time he was diagnosed.

I talked before about timing and divine intervention. Well, this moment was another time. We were only moments away from strapping him into his car seat and whisking him away from the very place that saved his life.

As it was, it required a team of professionals who rushed to his side just to keep him breathing and stabilize him. If it had happened in the car or during the night, he would have died. He was so silent during the seizure that I would have never heard anything on his monitor to alert me of the danger. He would have certainly slipped away during the night. I thought of both of these scenarios so many times. I *knew* God had had a hand in revealing this tumor and latest trial so that he would *not* be taken from us. Once again, even though I hated the new bump in the road, it was one more miracle we were privileged to experience.

CB Entry: Monday, May 17, 2010, 7:38 p.m.

Wishing the news I have was better, but Logan relapsed. He woke up Sunday morning with a fever of 102, so we took him to Lehigh Valley Hospital. Blood cultures were drawn to test for infection. Since his counts were good, they were going to discharge us and notify us concerning the cultures.

As we were being discharged, Logan suffered a seizure. We were immediately taken to the PICU for further testing and a CAT scan, which showed a tumor on the brain. We are waiting for surgery in the morning, which just happens to be his second birthday. Please pray that his surgery goes well, that he recovers quickly, and that he suffers no damage due to the removal of the tumor.

CB Entry: Tuesday, May 18, 2010, 5:24 p.m.

Logan's surgery started at 9:30 and finished at 4:30. He is doing well and already trying to sit up. The nurses are going to keep him sedated until the MRI tomorrow. The surgeon (Dr. Camici) felt confident that he removed the entire tumor but still recommends radiation at that spot.

His color looks very good. The CT scan of his chest/abdomen/pelvis was all clear, no tumors! We should have bone marrow results at the end of the week. We hope to extubate him tomorrow after the MRI if his vitals remain stable. Even though it's been a long day, it feels good to see him fighting the nurses to wake up. Thank you for all the thoughts and prayers today, and please continue to pray for him!

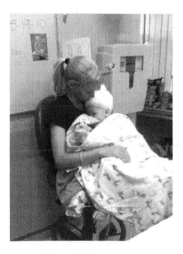

CB Entry: Wednesday, May 19, 2010, 7:03 p.m.

My baby is back in my arms again! They kept Logan sedated all evening into this morning until they did the MRI at 9 a.m. Dr. Camici looked at the MRI and was very happy with it—no signs of the tumor.

They weaned him off the respirator and saw he was breathing on his own. They extubated him around noon. They then took out 2 of his IVs, and I was able to finally hold him. He was able to move both legs and arms and open both eyes, which is a great sign after this type of surgery. They also removed his catheter, and he has been able to fill many diapers on his own. So he is slowing getting rid of all the excess fluids and puffiness from surgery.

As of 4:00 p.m. today, he was able to have clear fluids and liquids, but he hasn't taken anything yet. He is still groggy and probably has a sore throat from the breathing tube. We are no longer heavily monitored, and they feel we should be able to move over to the pediatric floor tomorrow.

We also talked to Dr. Kushner from Sloan and are getting more information on the new protocol that will include some chemo, some radiation, and some 3F8 to ensure no more tumors will develop in the brain. We are confident with the results of the past cases that have participated in this protocol.

The preliminary results from Logan's bone marrow have come back clear, and with the clear CT scan from yesterday, it shows that the 3F8 is working.

Another point to mention is that some kids do relapse with tumors in the brain due to the fact that the chemo/3F8 that we have done before does not pass the barrier into the brain. The chemo with the new protocol is specifically designed to reach the brain, and the 3F8 will be administered via his new Ommaya reservoir they inserted under his scalp during surgery. This Ommaya reservoir is similar to the port in his chest. It can be accessed with a needle and the medicine can be directly injected in. Please pray that Logan will continue to heal so well and resume all normal two-year-old activities. Hopefully, we'll be able to enjoy some time at home before heading to Sloan.

CB Entry: Thursday, May 20, 2010, 7:57 p.m.

Logan ended up eating some baby food pears last night, which was so comforting to see. He ate some more at breakfast and has been drinking from his sippy cup like a champ. He has been pretty sleepy today, which is understandable after all he's been through. He was able to sit up on his own and eat a bunch of strawberries sent from his Mimi.

They did an EEG test today. This is where they monitor his brain and check for any signs of seizures. We should have those results tomorrow. He is on and will stay on an anti-seizure medicine for a while just to be on the safe side. They moved us from the PICU to the pediatric floor today. Never thought I would be so happy to be back on this part of the hospital, but I am.

It sounds like they'll be discharging us tomorrow. Since Logan handled the surgery so well, they feel comfortable with sending him home to recover until he starts the next treatment. We are still talking to several doctors to see if we will be returning to Sloan for more treatment or coming back to Lehigh Valley for them to follow Sloan's protocol. Dr. Kushner feels comfortable with either, so we are just having the radiation specialists get together and talk. We should know more tomorrow.

We are hoping to have next week off to just have Logan recover from surgery before starting anything. The only thing we would have next week is a radiation simulation. Well, I thought "diagnosis week" back in August was the *worst* week of my life. This might take the cake on that one. We were so close to having our "normal life" back that it really hit us hard.

The unknown is always scary, and knowing Logan will have more treatments ahead of him has just broken my heart. *But* we have so much faith and know God has been with us each and day and minute. We are thankful for so many things. We are thankful that his seizure happened in the hospital and not at home or in the middle of the night. We were literally getting our discharge papers when it happened, and I know God was watching over that.

We are also thankful that he handled the surgery so amazingly. Once again, the staff laughs about how *strong* and *amazing* he is, and that is what is getting him through this. We are also thankful for all other scans to be clear. We are also thankful for our family and friends for their continued love and support. I could not be doing this without them and love you all so much.

A special thanks to my hubby for asking all the questions and helping through the hard times when I just freeze up. He is a great daddy and husband for me to lean on.

Please pray for Logan's recovery and for our next treatment steps to be made clear. Looking forward to having my family together tomorrow.

To say we were shocked by this relapse is an understatement for the whole family. Diagnosis was hard, but a relapse seemed impossible. It gave us *no* hope for a future with Logan. It was Logan's second birthday, and he was scheduled for brain surgery. Are you kidding me? I still look back at that time as a sick joke. I always try to look at the positive side of every situation, so I praised God that the surgery had gone well. I also looked at it as if he'd be tumor free on his birthday, which was an amazing gift. How else can you look at it? What other choice do you have? Of course it is horrific and sounds like a lifetime movie that couldn't possibly be real. But it was. It was our reality!

We had Logan's birthday cake outside his PICU room. He was heavily sedated; his nurse was a strict guard, which was good. She watched Logan like a hawk and wanted no noise to stimulate him. Even though he had been heavily sedated, if he heard our voices, he would get agitated and try to sit up and move—typical behavior for my little fighter. He had enough sedation to put a horse down, but he was still fighting. Of course, the nurse wanted to keep him calm so he wouldn't wake and pull his breathing tube out. So we tried to celebrate as much as we could as my baby lay in a hospital bed heavily sedated with his arms and legs restrained.

While trying to enjoy his cake, we decided to give some slices to other patients and parents on the floor. One patient was a little girl who had ruptured her spleen during a softball game. Jason carried a piece of Logan's birthday cake to her father. They exchanged stories, and the girl's father just looked shocked and in disbelief. I am sure they left the PICU floor thankful for their own situation after hearing our story. I had just wished our situation wasn't the worst case on that floor. At that time, it was. My hope was that soon it *wouldn't* be.

In the darkness of a very difficult night after an agonizingly long day, I was crying hysterically and praying to God for understanding and for strength to keep going because I felt my courage slipping away. How could God allow this to happen to people much less children? How could he sit back and watch as my son was suffering and could possibly die? It finally hit me. In that dark hour of despair, I had clarity. God *had* gone through the same thing. He watched his own dear son, Jesus, suffer and be crucified on the cross. At that moment, I realized God wasn't having us go through anything he hadn't. He knew *just* how I felt. Though I still felt horrible, I knew he was watching over us. He felt my pain. He had been there, and I would still pray for a miracle that Logan would pull through this. Even with all his suffering, it did give me comfort, and for that I was very thankful.

Brain surgery had been on May 18, 2010 (Logan's second birthday). He started seventeen days of radiation on May 27. He had full brain and spine radiation and then what they call a "boost" treatment

51

of radiation right to the spot where the tumor was. They also did two cycles of low-dose chemo followed by a set of scans on July 14. All Logan's scans came back clear, and he was set up to do 8H9, the version of 3F8 specifically for the brain. The 8H9 process was a much simpler than the 3F8 process. The 8H9 was injected directly into his brain via the port they had inserted during the brain tumor resection. No pain or side effects, so it was a relatively easy process.

Once again, he was in remission. It was an extremely happy place, but we weren't sitting as comfortably as we had been the first time. We knew it might not last. Logan might have to fight the beast again.

CB Entry: June 1, 2010, 8:08 p.m.

What a *wonderful* weekend. We had Logan's birthday celebration on Saturday. It was so great to share that special day with family and friends. Seeing Logan dig into his cake with his hands was as it should have been.

The past couple of days, Logan has had really good mornings and evenings but some spells in the afternoon. Even though he can't tell us what is bothering him, he just wasn't feeling good. He ate great all weekend and is back to sleeping well now that he's off the steroids, which Mommy is totally enjoying.

Logan also had no more fevers since that one on Thursday night, and we praise God for that. God gave us an amazing weekend at home with family and friends, and for that, we thank him. It totally recharges my mommy battery to be home in a "normal" setting with loved ones.

We are back at Sloan this week, Tuesday thru Friday. We got in early this morning for radiation at 7:40. It went good, and when he woke up, we headed to the clinic for Logan's chemo. It was done in an hour, and Logan slept through the whole thing. He ended up sleeping most of the afternoon too, and when he woke up, I took him for a walk around the city. It was so beautiful out, and the fresh air does us both good.

He ate a *huge* dinner and enjoyed playing our game of throwing stuff off the table and laughing hysterically. Hearing his belly laugh just warms my heart. Logan also had no vomiting today, which is such a blessing. Even though it is hard to be back here and going through more treatments, we have to focus on all the positive things God is showing us.

Please pray that Logan's radiation and chemo treatments will do their job and have *no* side effects. Also, pray that Logan will continue to eat up a storm and have no vomiting or diarrhea. We did start him today on an antibiotic to hopefully prevent any diarrhea he might have from the chemo. So far so good.

Chapter 7

REARING ITS UGLY HEAD AGAIN

After Logan was in remission for another nine months, our world was tossed upside down again. He had scans in February 2011, and the preliminary results were looking good. The only thing we were waiting for was the bone marrow biopsy. Thinking he was in the clear and celebrating another three months of remission, we got a call from Sloan. I remember being at an OfficeMax at that moment printing off Logan's Caring Bridge journals. There I was, trying to document my son's courageous journey when I learned his journey was far from over.

I saw I had missed a call from Sloan. My heart dropped. What did they want? Why were they calling us now? When I called the office back, the secretary said that Dr. Kushner was talking to Jason. I *knew* that wasn't good. You never want to talk to the doctor, because that means something has come up.

Those next couple of minutes were pure anguish until I could talk to Jason. As soon as he picked up, he started talking about what Dr. Kushner had told him, but then he broke down. We met at my parents' house, where Logan and Jeffrey were playing. Within minutes, Jason's parents were also there. I sat there in shock and disbelief. I was looking at how great he looked on the outside, but I knew his cancer was growing again.

At that moment, all I could remember were the statistics. Neuroblastoma can be cured as long as there is no relapse. If there is a relapse, a brain relapse is considered better then a relapse in the rest of the body. Logan's first relapse had been in the brain. Technically, the brain was untouched by any of the chemo's we had done up until this point because those therapies don't pass the blood brain barrier. The brain is not off limit to neuroblastoma cells. Now to have a reoccurrence in his body after he had received treatment to that part was considered *incurable*. How do you process that? How do you even deal with that? How do you stay positive through that?

Around that time, my husband's grandfather had passed away. As if a death in our family wasn't depressing enough, we felt as if we had just been given a death sentence of our own due to Logan's relapse. All the other siblings had a sitter for their kids so they could say good-bye to their grandfather at the funeral. I could have had the boys with someone else, but I just couldn't do it. I needed them there. I couldn't bear to sit at a funeral. I needed the distraction of my boys to break my thoughts of perhaps having to sit in that same church for Logan's funeral. As awful as it was, I had my moments of utter loss and had to fight the depressing thoughts of that pressing possibility. Staying positive isn't always easy. At that point, we really did think things were hopeless.

While we mourned the loss of our beloved grandfather (pictured above with Logan and his Mom Mom), I simply tried to focus on Logan playing and asking for constant snacks because I didn't want to let myself go into those dark places concerning our future. The distraction helped me from having my mind fly to the unthinkable, the unimaginable. When those who have lived long, happy lives die, you rejoice in what they had accomplished. Though you miss them, you reflect on their lives and savor your memories of them. But when children die, that doesn't happen. They were not supposed to die young and be laid to rest before their parents. They are not to have all those memories stolen. Their deaths leave no comfort. It makes no sense to me and it never will.

CB Entry: Thursday, February 24, 2011, 2:27 p.m.

Right when we think we could breathe for a bit, we get another shock. Logan's results came back on the bone marrow, and one of the samples taken showed neuroblastoma cells.

We will go to LV clinic tomorrow to check Logan's counts and get the all- clear to head back to New York next week for 5 days of chemo. After that, we will do an infusion to give Logan his stem cells that we harvested months ago on the following Monday.

We are also mourning the loss of our beloved Pop Pop Snyder this week, so to say when it rains, it pours is about right. I really don't have much else to say right now. This has hit me really hard, and I guess I am still in shock and utter disappointment. But I did want to make sure I updated everyone since you have been so supportive. Please pray.

CB Entry: February 28, 2011, 2:18 p.m.

Today, we are in New York early to start Logan's chemo week. Mimi and Jeffrey came in with Jason and me. The boys did great all morning in the playroom. We started with fluids first to make sure Logan was well hydrated, and then the chemo around 2:00. Today he is getting Carboplatin, Irinotecan, and Temozolomode (oral). Logan will also be going back to the Ronald with a fluid bag on him so that he continues to push the chemo out. They don't want it staying in his kidneys or liver to do any damage, so they must keep him super hydrated.

It was really nice to finally sit down with Dr. Kushner and Nurse Practitioner Kristina and get our game plan for the week. It has been a horrible couple of days with the new adjustment of a relapse, but we have picked ourselves up and are ready to fight again and continue to pray for strength and healing from God. Jason, Jeffrey, and Mimi will be heading home tonight, but we have enjoyed the time with them today.

They have also drawn a HAMA sample, which will be tested tomorrow. We will find out on Wednesday if he is HAMA negative. Hoping that he is so that we can continue with treatment once Logan bounces back from this week.

Please pray that Logan will have a good week and stay strong through this chemo. Also pray the chemo will do its job to clean out the bone marrow of any neuroblastoma cells. Pray for no side effects and remission once more. Above all, pray for a cure!

CB Entry: March 1, 2011, 1:49 p.m.

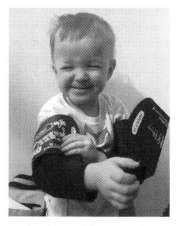

Last night, Logan did great. He ate a good dinner with Jason, Mimi, and Jeffrey. He went right to bed and slept great all night. I did change him several times during the night since he is on fluids and he fills those diapers quickly.

He woke up happy, and we were back at Sloan around 9 this morning. The picture taken today shows Logan happy and doing his own blood pressure. He knows the drill! His chemo is all done for today, and we are on the 4 hours of fluids before we can leave. Even though he leaves the hospital on the fluid bag, they require 4 hours done here since it is a faster rate than the backpack we take with us.

Today's chemo was the same as yesterday—Carboplatin, Irinotecan, and Temozolomode. Logan is napping now and hopefully will wake up feeling well.

It has been a hard day knowing my sister is in labor with my niece and I'm not able to be there with her. Never have I wanted to be in two places at once more than now—just another part of this cancer world that sucks. I am trying to focus on the important thing that Brandy has a safe delivery of a healthy baby and Logan handles this chemo amazingly. The cousins will meet this weekend, and I cannot wait.

Praying for another good night for Logan and for the chemo to do its job with no side effects. Praying for remission and a cure!

CB Entry: March 2, 2011, 1:13 p.m.

Logan had another good night, even with the 2-hour trip to urgent care. Logan's fluid bag kept alarming "high pressure"; that usually means there is a kink in the tubing or something obstructing the flow. I check everywhere and couldn't find what was causing it. So we headed to urgent care so they could fix it. Logan had been playing like a mad man in the playroom, so I thought maybe one of his needles wasn't in place in his port.

Once we got there, it was a good 2 hours before the nurse could see us. She carefully looked under the dressing of his port and saw that both his needles were in place. Logan was super excited to not have to be reaccessed, as was I. So she just switched the fluid to be connected to the other side of his port, and that worked. We have no idea why it did that, but were happy it was resolved. We were on our way and back to the Ronald by 10. Logan had a very restful night and woke up happy.

We had a wonderful visit with Mimi, Pappy, and Jeffrey today. It really helps to break up the week, and Logan was so excited to see them. Logan's chemo is done for the day. Today, he had the Irinotecan, Temozolomode (he had both on Monday and Tuesday), and a different one called Etoposide. So far so good. He had a little spell where he was lying on me and didn't want to eat lunch, but he soon snapped out of it and was back to playing and eating lots of fruit.

Praying for another playful, hungry, and restful night. Also praying the chemo is effective with *no* side effects. Praying for a cure!

Chapter 8

KNOCKED DOWN
BUT NOT OUT

Logan had had two relapses in eighteen months, and we were doing everything our medical facility recommended, which included such toxic choices as chemotherapy, radiation, 3F8, and 8H9. From his diagnosis date, Logan had relapsed nine months later in the brain and then nine months in the bone marrow. Trusting in the medical community was not giving Logan good health or a cure. In fact, once neuroblastoma patients relapse, they are considered incurable in the medical world. *Incurable?* What a horrible word that sucks all faith, hope, and courage out of a soul.

A friend and fellow oncology mom, Annabeth, gave me a wonderful thought and insight. She said if you're driving in a car and it breaks down once, you have your mechanic fix it. If it continues to break down, maybe you need to find another mechanic. Realizing our medical team had no options for us that were working to keep Logan in remission, we began a desperate search for other alternatives.

That's when our natural journey really began. We desperately needed some help at that point, and we thankfully received guidance that proved to be Logan's salvation. Esther and her husband, John, from Michigan, a couple with miracles working in their own lives, happened to stop by my parents' home. They had been visiting a mutual friend in the area and needed to borrow a tool. After my parents had brought them up to date on Logan's journey, they began to relate a cancer story of their own. I unexpectedly dropped in just at that moment and was able to hear her miraculous success story firsthand. Esther and I were so excited to get started on a plan for Logan that she called her naturalist and handed me the phone. We were ready to forge ahead before we all had to face one more setback.

I feel that that day was divine intervention in our lives; I believe the information, our connection, and our decisions that day saved Logan's life. Here is Esther's miraculous story.

My diagnosis was a hernia in the groin—so I thought okay, I'll do the surgery. Slowly waking up from the anesthesia, I could see from my husband's face that the diagnosis was *cancer!* When I was fully awake, he told me I had non-Hodgkin's lymphoma. Well, the roller-coaster of emotions began. Sadness, helplessness, feeling sorry for myself, anger—you name it, I had it.

My husband had some of it too. My children were still young and in school, so now how to tell them? Right off, I knew that I wasn't going to do chemo—I knew too many people who had died as a result of chemo and radiation, and that was totally off my radar. My sister had had radiation and she was left with bad scarring in her lungs, so *no way* was I going to submit to any of that.

My husband wanted me to do the chemo, *but* my daughter went to the library and brought home many books about my disease and chemo and radiation. After reading for himself, he knew why had I made my decision. He understood me when I said just let me die because I wouldn't do chemo or radiation.

So my husband and two girls said just feed us the way you have to eat. That was so great because I didn't have to worry about making accommodations for two meals.

In the beginning, I didn't know what I was doing—I just knew I had to quit animal protein and sugar since these two things feed cancer. I didn't know about the dairy at the time. So being Italian, I still enjoyed my cheeses—not good!

I started the alternative route—You have to be careful here because some out there aren't for real. But with my heavenly Father's help through lots of time on our knees, my husband and I got answers every step of the way. The alternative world today is awesome—not like it was back in the 90s.

I started with hydrocolon therapy, eating more raw, and learning a whole new world of healthy eating. I started exercising more regularly—learning, learning, learning.

Then we had a big, horrible, stress come into our lives as I was diagnosed again, but instead of the tumor being marble size, it was baseball size. No way to have surgery again. So more research, and again, our heavenly Father always comes through. A friend had survived colon cancer. She recommended I go see the doctor she worked with. So I went through 4 months of a juice diet at a clinic outside of Seattle. There, I learned that dairy was also an enemy to my body while trying to fight cancer, so off dairy I went. I kept that diet for a year on my own.

Then a chiropractor friend from Portland, Oregon, said to come see him and he would try to help me. My week with him gave wonderful results, but he said I really had to find someone close to me that does electro-thermal therapy because it would be difficult for me to fly to Oregon regularly.

Again, my God found someone 3 hours away, and I finally was able to kick the tumor and the cancer cells.

It has been 10 years now, but I have been cancer free for 8 years now, well into my 9th year. By his grace I am thriving. At first, many thought I was crazy with the choices I made, but now, many want to do it my way and ask for my help, which I am happy to give.

Chapter 9

THROUGH THE EYES
OF A NATURALIST

After hearing Esther's story, a lightbulb went on in my mind and was guiding us down a new path and showing us some hope we so desperately needed. We felt compelled to meet Flora and get some direction for healing, so we made plans to meet her.

Sitting with Flora was much different from sitting with our medical team. All her suggestions were natural and healing. She gave us a lot of information to process but no promises. She said there were many things we could do to help heal the body and then build it up to fight the cancer on its own. Of course, sometimes, even when we try it all, our outcome might not be what we want. She reminded us that Logan had had a lot of treatment already for a little boy and that God was really the one who could overrule our efforts. It was hard to hear that but oh so true.

She said when dealing with a young child, we have to get creative on how we get all this *good* fuel into him. He probably wouldn't be able to do as strict of a detox as her older patients did, but we would do what we could.

Flora gave us information about three main avenues of healing. They included a special diet, supplemental drops, and use of the Rife machine. Together, those three would build his body to fight the cancer, heal his body from past treatments, and hopefully keep him in remission.

Chapter 10

THE CANCER DIET

What we eat fuels our bodies. What we eat fuels what is inside our body as well. What we put in measures what we get out. This is what any health coach or nutritionist will tell you.

One pressing fact to always remember is that cancer cells feed on sugar. Even our medical doctors will admit this. A PET scan involves the injection of radioactive isotopes. What the doctors are looking for determines which isotope is injected. If they are looking for cancer, they will send a FDG, molecule, a modified form of glucose. When tissues absorb a lot of glucose, that may indicate a cancerous tumor.

So if we all know that, and it has been scientifically proven, wouldn't it make sense to limit our intake of sugar and make our bodies uninviting environments for cancer? This diet limits sugar intake and thus makes the body more alkaline than acidic. (Chapter 11 goes into further detail about the importance of this.) It's possible to control alkalinity by the foods we eat.

I talked in the beginning about doing natural things and buying all organic foods for the boys. Unfortunately, I didn't have the knowledge at that time of *what* natural and organic foods Logan should have. Just because it was organic didn't mean it was what Logan's body needed to keep him in remission. We researched the ketogenic diet, a low-carb/high-fat diet that starves cancer cells of sugar and poisons them with ketones. We also researched the Budwig diet of consuming cottage cheese and flaxseed oil in preventing and curing cancer and chronic diseases. We just were trying to explore all our options out there and see their reasoning behind them.

Our diet from Flora is what I like to call the raw cancer diet. It also happens to be the diet that Johns Hopkins Hospital recommends for cancer patients. It consists of fresh, raw vegetables and fruits, raw seeds and nuts, and whole grains, and it limits meat to only chicken occasionally and some kosher fish. Kosher is important because you know the food much comply with a strict policy of kosher food laws, including cleanliness, purity and quality. Animal protein, dairy, bread, and pasta are just a few of the things to avoid. That sounds like a rough list, but there are many delicious substitutes I've found.

Here are some of the basics of this diet.

1. **No dairy.** Dairy can cause mucus and inflammation. Avoiding inflammation in the body is very important. Inflammation creates more work for the body. You can have swelling in your blood vessels, tissue, and organs. Inflammation can lead to disease, so it is important to avoid that.

2. **Limit meats.** Red meats can be acidic; however, red meat and fish provide iron. Once Logan was in remission, we introduced some red meat and fish occasionally. Red meat is also hard to digest because it has more fat. If you eat red meat, it should definitely be organic, hormone free.

   It also takes more enzymes to break down meat. You want enzymes to break up such things as cancer or disease and not be busy breaking up food. These are just a couple of reasons to limit red meat and fish to keep the body alkaline (see chapter 11).

3. **No soy products.** Soy is an estrogen producer; it can be a driver for breast or cervix cancer. Cancer patients and females should avoid it. Also, there are GMOs (genetically modified organisms) in soy. GMOs are chemical induced, so you don't know how your body will react to them.

4. **No breads or white pasta.** White bread and pasta are made with white flour, which turns into sugar in the body. Once

again, you're trying to limit sugar intake, so cutting these out is important. It almost turns into glue, basically like when you add water to flour. You certainly don't want glue-like substances in your body.

5. **Limit fruits with high sugar content**. Some fruits have more sugar than others, so even fruit has to be limited or watched. Refined or processed sugar is the worst, because the body cannot break it down, but your body can break down the natural sugar found in fruits.

I went online to check sugar content in fruits. While Logan was fresh into remission, I really limited the fruits that had higher sugar content. Below is a chart that shows the sugar content in some fruit my boys like. I really tried to stay in the green and avoid the red section or at least just serve them occasionally. There are many sources online to check fruit options and sugar content. It is important that the body gets a variety of fruit by not eating the same fruits every day or only those that have lower sugar content. Your body needs the benefits each fruit offers. There are great charts available online that indicate which fruits are very rich in antioxidants. It is very interesting to see how the deeper-colored fruits and vegetables contain higher antioxidant levels. Even though grapes are high in sugar, they do have excellent health benefits.

Sugar Content	Fruit
fruits low to medium high in sugar	cantaloupe
	strawberries
	papaya
	peaches
	nectarines
	honeydew melons

	apricots
	grapefruit
	watermelon
	blueberries
	apples
fruits fairly high in sugar	plums
	oranges
	pears
	pineapple
	kiwi
fruits very high in sugar	grapes
	figs
	bananas
	dried fruit (dates, raisins, prunes)
	tangerines
	cherries

It can be very overwhelming to make such changes to your diet. At first, I didn't even know where to start. So I started slow. I cut out major things first. Since cancer feeds off sugar, that is perhaps the most important to control. Then I cut out all milk, cheese, and red meat. I found some good substitutes that helped make it feel we had something similar to eat.

Once we adjusted to that, I focused on making Logan's lunches mainly raw. We do *all* raw lunches, and it is the best meal he gets. If we could eat raw all day, we would, but I also realize I am working with a child. If you understand these foods will make you feel good and even beat cancer, wouldn't you eat them? I realized that no matter how beneficial the foods were, if he didn't eat them, we wouldn't be making any progress. To my surprise, Logan accepted the new diet, and now, he actually chooses healthy foods over those less so. It seems his body knows what it needs and what makes him feel better.

Over the years, Logan's lunches have changed to whatever his tastes were. His lunch lists varies, but it includes raw carrots, raw beets (shredded), red pepper, cucumbers, some type of bean (his favorites are chickpeas and aduki beans), hard-boiled eggs, and some type of fruit, including blueberries, cantaloupe, or watermelon. He then sprinkles celery salt, sesame seeds, and flaxseed oil all over his lunch. I let him do it himself, and he loves it. Each and every day it's the same raw foods, and he devours them.

I was worried about Logan starting kindergarten and how I would control his healthy lunches outside my house. I was concerned that other students would make comments about what he ate because it was certainly different from typical school lunches. Logan can be very sensitive to what others say, but this was a learning process. I knew that above all, I had to instill in all my children that this was a better way to live and eat. If we continue on this path, we will grow strong and healthy and stay out of the hospital.

Helping Logan deal with his differences was very important for me. One thing that has helped him was talking with him about food allergies. Many children, even Logan's cousin Sophia, have nut allergies. So there are certain things she can't eat; if she does, they make her sick. Some kids are allergic to milk products. Once I really focused on that with Logan, he seemed to understand and accept it more. He saw that he wasn't the only one who had to avoid certain foods.

So we played around with what I packed in his lunch until we found a good combination. One time, Logan asked me to pack some raw beets in his lunch. I was hesitant because I knew those were very different and could get messy, but I sent them. A few days later, I could tell something was bothering him. He got all upset when I would make his lunch in the morning. He finally broke down and told me someone had made fun of his beets and accused him of eating worms. My heart broke for him. I hated seeing him upset and hated the fact even more that he had felt singled out. I sometimes wish we could just put our children in little bubbles and keep them safe and protected, but I realize that's just part of life and growing up. These life experiences, as tough as they are, will shape and mold Logan into who he will become.

The raw lunches (above) were the easy part for us. The hardest part for me was dinner. It was challenging to have to cut my meals down by not using red meat, pasta, white potatoes, or dairy and to satisfy not only my children but also my husband. Luckily, I was put in touch with a great guy who happens to be a personal trainer and vegan. He and his wife had a plethora of amazing recipes they passed along to me that I'm passing along to you in Chapter 31.

It's easy to list the things you should be eating but a lot harder to come up with good-tasting meals the whole family will enjoy. So it was very helpful to have those recipes to try with my family. If you need to change your diet, seek out a vegetarian or vegan friend for recipes. A health coach is also a great resource for direction in meal planning. For this cancer diet, the basic idea is the more raw and plant-based the better. Having someone who can balance it out to get enough protein as well is important. There are many plant-based proteins that are easier to digest than meats.

So now you know the foods we have avoided or limited. Finding alternatives, which you can enjoy, is possible. Here is a list of substitutes we use every day.

Food	Substitute (brand name)
bread	Ezekiel 4:9
butter	Earth Balance (soy-free buttery spread)
cheese	Daiya
chicken nuggets	Quorn/Chik'n Nuggets
flour	King Arthur flour, gluten-free, multipurpose rice flour
hot dogs	Lightlife/Smart Dogs
milk	Blue Diamond/Almond Breeze (unsweetened)
	coconut milk
pasta	Ancient Harvest/quinoa pasta (gluten free)
	Ronzoni (gluten free)
sweetener	agave nectar

Find a grocery store with a good organic section. You might also be interested in joining a Community Supportive Agriculture (CSA) organization. It's a wonderful way to get fresh, local fruits and vegetables. Your membership fee entitles you to local produce as it is harvested. To find a CSA near you, visit www.orbit.org.

Not only have we changed what we eat, we have also changed what we drink. Water is so important; our bodies are composed of 60 percent water, which is necessary for digestion, absorption, circulation, making saliva, moving nutrients, and maintaining body temperature. All those functions are crucial for living. Water helps energize your muscles and helps make your skin look good. Water helps your kidneys, which transports waste products out of cells. As if you couldn't tell, you *need* water to live, so you need to drink enough water, and you have to make sure your water is pure.

We had our water tested for bacteria and chlorine. Our naturalist reviewed our water report because I wasn't sure what I was looking at, but the staff from the water company was very helpful. They can guide you if any levels look too high. If so, they might suggest you shock your system. Shock chlorination is a simple way to disinfect your domestic drinking water when it is contaminated with bacteria. It introduces very high levels of chlorine into your water system. Fortunately, our water was in good levels so we didn't have to consider this process.

It is also important to have no soda; there's nothing but added sugar. We all get enough sugar in our diets we cannot avoid, and this is one way to avoid unnecessary sugar. Drink only pure water; your water could be acidic, so it's important to do some research to find a good water ionizer and purifier. Making your body alkaline with your food and water is critical. Water ionizers do a great job of alkalizing your water. There are many different prices, levels, and brands of ionizing water systems to choose from. The water you drink is just as important as the food you eat.

Chapter 11

THE MIRACLE OF ALKALINITY

All diseases thrive in acidic systems. Cancer cells grow in acidic environments but cannot in alkaline environments, so it makes sense to make sure your body is alkaline.

When we first tested Logan, he was acidic—shock! No wonder cancer cells could grow in him; they had the perfect environment. So we began to reverse this by giving him all alkalizing foods. Now it's a balance—he can have some acidic foods, but checking his pH is critical to making sure he stays in that good range. All foods whether acid or alkaline, offer benefits to your body. You don't want to just eat alkaline foods for this reason. It is a delicate balance of eating both to reap all their benefits, but maintaining your personal pH level in the alkaline range. So the idea is you can eat some acidic foods, but not too many to change your body's pH away from Alkaline.

The pH scale ranges from 0 to 14; 7 is the halfway point where there is a balance between acidity and alkalinity. A pH of 7 is considered neutral, and the most optimal pH zone is between 6.75 and 7.25. We test Logan's pH by having him urinate on pH test strips. This is one thing that is easy to control daily. If we see he's out of range even a little bit, we balance it out by the foods we give him. There are also drops available online to help you achieve balance. I've used his diet to balance Logan. It is most helpful to use a chart that labels acid and alkaline foods. Several such charts are available online. I found this one below at www.billschoolcraft.com/ph/.

Most Alkaline	Alkaline	Lowest Alkaline	FOOD CATEGORY	Lowest Acid	Acid	Most Acid
Stevia	Maple Syrup, Rice Syrup	Raw Honey, Raw Sugar	SWEETENERS	Processed Honey, Molasses	White Sugar, Brown Sugar	NutraSweet, Equal, Aspartame, Sweet 'N Low
Lemons, Watermelon, Limes, Grapefruit, Mangoes, Papayas	Dates, Figs, Melons, Grapes, Papaya, Kiwi, Berries, Apples, Pears, Raisins	Oranges, Bananas, Cherries, Pineapple, Peaches, Avocados	FRUITS	Plums, Processed Fruit Juices	Sour Cherries, Rhubarb	Blueberries, Cranberries, Prunes
Asparagus, Onions, Vegetable Juices, Parsley, Raw Spinach, Broccoli, Garlic	Okra, Squash, Green Beans, Beets, Celery, Lettuce, Zucchini, Sweet Potato, Carob	Carrots, Tomatoes, Fresh Corn, Mushrooms, Cabbage, Peas, Potato Skins, Olives, Soybeans, Tofu	BEANS VEGETABLES LEGUMES	Cooked Spinach, Kidney Beans, String Beans	Potatoes (without skins), Pinto Beans, Navy Beans, Lima Beans	Chocolate
	Almonds	Chestnuts	NUTS SEEDS	Pumpkin Seeds, Sunflower Seeds	Pecans, Cashews	Peanuts, Walnuts
Olive Oil	Flax Seed Oil	Canola Oil	OILS	Corn Oil		
		Amaranth, Millet, Wild Rice, Quinoa	GRAINS CEREALS	Sprouted Wheat Bread, Spelt, Brown Rice	White Rice, Corn, Buckwheat, Oats, Rye	Wheat, White Flour, Pastries, Pasta
			MEATS	Venison, Cold Water Fish	Turkey, Chicken, Lamb	Beef, Pork, Shellfish
	Breast Milk	Soy Cheese, Soy Milk, Goat Milk, Goat Cheese, Whey	EGGS DAIRY	Eggs, Butter, Yogurt, Buttermilk, Cottage Cheese	Raw Milk	Cheese, Homogenized Milk, Ice Cream
Herb Teas, Lemon Water	Green Tea	Ginger Tea	BEVERAGES	Tea	Coffee	Beer, Soft Drinks

I test Logan's urine with the pH strips in the morning periodically. If he's more on the acidic side, I refer to the chart and feed him only alkaline foods to bring him back into balance. Maintaining alkalinity is a delicate balance that can be controlled by diet.

Outside the body, lemon juice is acidic (pH is below 7). However, inside the body, when lemon juice has been fully metabolized and its minerals are dissociated in the bloodstream, its effect is alkalizing and therefore raises the pH of body tissue (pH above 7). Since lemons are extremely alkalizing to the body, I squeeze half of one in a glass with a little water in the morning. Lemon water is the most alkaline and is a simple way to bring him back to alkaline or keep him there. I don't put lemon in all his water because lemons can harm tooth enamel. Lord knows, Logan has enough dental issues due to the chemo, so once a day is sufficient. The rest of the day, we just use pure water from our water ionizer.

Chapter 12

THE RIFE MACHINE

Another crucial part of our natural healing plan is the Rife machine. Royal Raymond Rife was an American inventor who in the 1930s invented what was called a Rife microscope. His microscope was able to see particles called "eberthella typhi," small turquoise bodies that weren't visible with the standard lab microscope. He also documented what was called the mortal oscillatory rate, which is being able to destroy organisms by vibrating them at a specific rate. Royal Rife never claimed he could cure cancer, but he did argue that he could "devitalize disease organisms" in live tissue "with certain exceptions." (Jones, Newell (1938-05-06). "Dread Disease Germs Destroyed By Rays, Claim of S.D. Scientist: Cancer Blow Seen After 18-Year Toil by Rife". San Diego Evening Tribune. p. 1.) The medical community ultimately discredited his works and claims. Although the medical community did not support his findings, the idea behind it made sense to us. At this point in Logan's journey, our medical community wasn't giving us the cure we needed so we needed to go elsewhere. The idea behind the Rife machine is that everything has a frequency that allows it to be broken apart, even cancer cells. The principle is similar to a singer who is able to break a glass if the pitch or frequency is high enough. Below is a picture of Logan wearing the machine.

We received helpful information about this machine from a naturalist, Flora, who is a licensed practitioner. She has done testing on Logan to evaluate his needs, including levels of metals in his body as well as things his body is lacking. We were able to receive a list of supplements he needs as well as information on how the Rife machine could be of help to Logan. It runs all night long and has several settings and frequencies programmed. It targets areas where cancer has been in Logan (brain, bone marrow, etc.). There are some other settings used to strengthen particular areas.

The Rife machine has settings to strengthen areas such as the kidneys. It can also be used to help eliminate things such as cramping, muscle twitching, or even certain parasites the body may be hosting. It can even be used to help balance body systems such as the muscular or lymphatic systems; it can be directed to any area and personalize the results.

We feel fortunate to have had Flora direct us since there are many types and brands of Rife machines. You can contact Flora at florawellness@yahoo.com. She is happy to share this information with anyone who feels he or she could benefit from such a machine.

Chapter 13

Supplements and Vitamins

Our naturalist Flora conducted advanced electro-dermal scanning, which is as noninvasive as you can get. Logan held onto a metal rod (slightly wet) while Flora used a metal probe and pushed gently on certain points on his other hand. Each point is connected to a different pathway of the body. Each point gave her a reading between one and ten, five being normal. If the levels are too low or too high, she made note of it. Based on those readings, she compiled a list of supplements to rid his body of bacteria or to build his body up with minerals he was lacking. Some supplements are for past treatment he has had, to rid his body of radiation and other harmful side effects. Others are to build up his immune system so if cancer cells pop up, his body will fight them on its own.

Finding a licensed practitioner who can calculate the proper dosages is critical. Their expertise is also very important in devising a program that will indeed heal the whole body and not be detrimental.

Flora was also able to test certain vitamins to determine their purity. Some we found to have impurities, including chlorine. We use mostly Amway vitamins based on her findings, including Nutrilite, a kid's chewable concentrated fruits and vegetables supplement; Nutrilite Multitarts, a chewable multivitamin; and Nutrilite chewable, a seasonal-strength probiotic. Other brands we order include Nature's Plus Calcium Children's Chewable Supplement Animal Parade and American Health Chewable Acidophilus and Bifidum.

We give these to all our children daily. It is important for all children to build their bodies up to fight colds and viruses. It is also essential to help with their growth.

Chapter 14

CRANIAL SACRAL THERAPY

Cranial sacral therapy is also something natural we started doing on our own to help Logan's healing and keep Logan's brain safe from any damage surgery and radiation have caused. When he started his treatments, he was very tight in his neck and shoulder area. His shoulders would tighten when he ran, and he actually favored one side. After a few treatments, he was more relaxed and was able to run with more freedom. It was quite a noticeable change.

Although we don't know what the treatments are doing on the inside, we were happy to see some results on the outside. We feel confident that these treatments won't hurt and can only help him in the long run. Logan seems to enjoy the treatments, and we are so happy to have some way to relax his taut muscles.

This is an actual testimonial from David, our cranial sacral therapist. He goes into details as to what cranial sacral therapy is and how it is benefiting Logan and so many others.

It has been a real pleasure doing craniosacral work with Logan. He is such a trusting, sensitive young man and seems to really understand what I am doing; he repositions his body from time to time to help me place my hands properly. He even sometimes seems to anticipate what I am going to do next and adjusts his body accordingly. In order for you to understand my work with Logan, I have to explain a little bit about the craniosacral system and how craniosacral therapy works.

Craniosacral therapy is a gentle touch therapy that enhances the functioning of the brain and spinal cord, relieves tension in the muscular system as well as in all connective tissue throughout the body, reduces neck and spinal tension, aids in circulation, generally improves organ function, and positively affects all other systems throughout the body.

Craniosacral therapy is based on the observation in the 1930s by osteopathic physician William Sutherland that the bones of the skull are designed to move and that gently adjusting the alignment of the bones had a therapeutic effect. Between 1975 and 1983 at Michigan State University, Dr. John Upledger, then clinical researcher and professor of biomechanics, and a team of anatomists, physiologists, biophysicists, and bioengineers conducted a number of scientific experiments to prove that the bones of the skull do indeed move; they recorded the therapeutic effects of craniosacral manipulation.

Upledger further developed what was then called cranial osteopathy to include the membranes that surround the brain and spinal cord. Significantly, he began to teach the technique he called craniosacral therapy to health care professionals and laypeople outside the osteopathic profession. In 1985, Dr. Upledger founded the Upledger Institute International, which has trained a hundred thousand people worldwide.

So let's take a look a little more deeply at how craniosacral therapy helps Logan maintain optimal brain function and health after recovery from brain surgery. Logan's brain needs a means of nourishment to carry on its metabolic functions, supply critical nutrients to the cells and many complex structures within the brain (such as the thalamus, hypothalamus, amygdala, etc.) and to remove toxins. These functions are especially important after the trauma of a brain tumor and subsequent surgery and chemotherapy. According to Upledger, the craniosacral system is largely responsible for this function. The brain and spinal cord are in fact a single organ separated only in medical dissections. Functionally, they are the same organ and constitute the central nervous system. The craniosacral system encloses the central nervous system with bone, membrane, and fluid.

The craniosacral system is composed of the skull and spine, the large triangular bone at the base of the spine called the sacrum, the membranes that surround the brain and spinal cord, and the fluid in the membranes. Logan's brain has a tough, relatively inelastic cover called the *dura mater* or simply dura. This membrane extends through an opening in the base of the skull to form the outer layer of the spinal cord through which nerves enter and exit along the spine. Cerebrospinal fluid, or CSF, which is critical for proper functioning of the central nervous system, is contained in these watertight membranes.

The skull or cranium is not composed of dry, brittle bones; instead, it is composed of pliable living tissue with soft connective tissue between the joints called sutures. In other words, the skull is resilient. The cranium is designed to have flexible sutures that absorb and redistribute forces or load placed on it and to accommodate fluid volume changes in the brain. When the movement of these bones is restricted, strain is placed upon the dural membrane, which can place pressure on and distortion in the brain tissue. A myriad of problems related to the function of the central nervous system can result. Likewise, internal strain on the dural membrane from trauma, disease, or surgery can cause restrictions in the bones, making it difficult for the skull to expand and contract to properly regulate the exchange of CSF and blood in the system.

As a therapist, my job is to palpate the regular ebb and flow of cerebrospinal fluid in the brain and spinal cord. This regular wave form of about 6 to 12 cycles per minute is called the craniosacral rhythm. There is a lot of controversy in the medical profession as to whether this rhythm actually exists as a separate and independent rhythm in its own right or is an aggregate of other wave forms in the body well known to medicine. Because this controversy is ongoing and unresolved, I will describe the Pressurestat model as developed by Dr. Upledger. Although this is just a model, it will at least give some sense of what I am feeling when I place my hands on Logan's head and body.

The Pressurestat model is based on the idea of a semi-closed hydraulic system with a regulated inflow and outflow of cerebrospinal fluid (CSF) in the craniosacral system. Because the fluid is incompressible, any pressure on the fluid anywhere in the system will be transmitted equally throughout the system. Imagine, for example, squeezing a water balloon. As the volume of cerebrospinal fluid in the craniosacral system rhythmically rises and falls, a very slight amount of movement between the joints of the cranial bones allows the skull to expand and contract to accommodate changes in fluid volume. The spinal cord expands and contracts as well transmitting the rhythm to the base of the spine at the sacrum.

This wave form is transmitted to the rest of the body according to Upledger's Pressurestat model via the motor nerves. Again, there are other theories about what is actually being felt and how the rhythm is generated. The important thing to recognize is that the rhythm exists and that palpating restrictions to the rhythm anywhere in body indicates the site of a problem that may be affecting the central nervous system. By using gentle touch, these restrictions can be removed, helping restore optimal function to the body's core physiological system.

The craniosacral system actually is more responsive to gentle touch than to heavy touch. When I palpate Logan's cranial rhythm, I start out with a pressure of about 5 grams, the weight of nickel, and increase that pressure very slowly until the resistance of the tissue is matched. More pressure or traction on the bones and membranes than that would cause the membranes to defensively contract. When I have the pressure just right, I can feel what the hydraulic system is doing under my hands, tension in the cranial bones, how the bones are moving or restricted, and the condition of the membranes attached to the cranial bones. Trusting what my hands are feeling, I follow whatever response the system provides and gently facilitate the body's natural tendency to correct itself.

As mentioned, Logan's brain is surrounded by a tough, relatively inelastic membrane called the dura mater. The dural membrane has two layers. These layers separate to form a sickle-shaped leaf from the inside of Logan's forehead to the back of his skull and a tent-like horizontal leaf that attaches to the bones on the side of his head where his ears are attached. This divides the brain roughly into quadrants.

Because CST increases fluid exchange in the brain, both blood and cerebrospinal fluid, it promotes clearing of toxins—cellular waste as well as debris from damaged cells—and increases the brain's supply of fresh fluids for healing and regeneration. Any tension, twisting, or adhesion of these membranes is necessarily going to have an effect on the form of the brain, possibly compressing the passageways for cerebrospinal fluid and blood, thus depriving the brain of its full measure of nourishment and cleansing.

It's safe to assume that Logan's brain tumor crowded the spaces in the brain and caused a distortion of the membranes. The surgery undoubtedly left some scar tissue. The port used to monitor Logan's cerebrospinal fluid and inject chemo had to penetrate the dural membrane. And because it has to be left permanently in Logan's brain, the port must also exert some strain and perhaps some twisting on Logan's dural membranes.

A big part of the cranial work I am doing with Logan is keeping the dural membrane as free of strain as possible so the craniosacral system can do its job. The dural membrane attaches to the inner side of the skull and to the membranes layers below it that attach to the brain. It is firmly attached at the opening at the base of skull that leads into the spinal cord. It then becomes the outer layer of the spinal cord attaching at a couple of places in the neck, and then hanging loose (to accommodate bending and twisting of the spine), until it reattaches at the second segment of the triangular bone at the base of the spine called the sacrum.

Even slight tension on the membranes can stress the entire central nervous system and cause numerous physical, mental, and emotional problems. There are also innumerable ways in which cranial nerves may be entrapped, causing symptoms such as headaches, dizziness, fatigue, poor attention, lack of persistence at tasks, poor short-term memory, impaired thinking, and problem solving.

Improving fluid motion and exchange in the craniosacral system specifically enhances the functions of the brain; spinal cord; autonomic control systems; visual, auditory, olfactory, and gustatory sensory systems; motor and motor coordination systems; the endocrine system; and the immune system, according to Dr. Upledger. From all this, it should be easy to see how important maintaining a healthy craniosacral system is for Logan's recovery from a brain tumor.

The first time I saw Logan, the bones of his skull were barely moving and the dural membranes were extremely tight. His head is slightly misshapen and looks a little like a parallelogram if you look very closely. Whether this is a result of the surgery or directly caused by the brain tumor I do not know. It is reasonable to assume, however, that the port permanently embedded in his brain would cause some amount of strain on Logan's brain. This lack of movement in the cranial bones and the tension on the membranes surely must have restricted the flow of CSF and blood in his brain and probably affected the spinal cord as well.

As I place my hands gently on Logan's head, I can feel how his cranial bones are moving and what kind of tension is exerted on the dural membranes. Using the bones as "handles," I can gently traction the dural membranes, follow the release of tension and adhesions, and untwist any distortion in the leaves of the membranes. As this occurs, I may feel a sudden pulsing of the craniosacral rhythm, which indicates that a restriction is being removed and something positive is happening. The less strain on the membranes and the more freely the bones move, the more I can sense the rhythmic rise and fall of CSF in Logan's brain, and I know something good is happening.

One of the functions of movable cranial sutures is to accommodate rapid brain growth in infancy and childhood. The skull bones in fact add new bone along the sutures in response to tension from the expanding dural membrane. If the bones are stuck or the membranes are strained and inhibiting brain growth—well, you can imagine what would happen. At Logan's age, it is critically important that that both the dural membranes and the cranial bones are able to accommodate the rapid growth of his brain.

Logan's cranial system was so tight on the first session that I wondered if anything positive had really happened by the end of the session, but a number of his relatives told me independently that they saw a remarkable change in him. His shoulders were no longer hunched up around his ears, and he seemed to be more vibrant and alive, running around and playing with more energy and excitement than they had ever seen.

The tension on Logan's skull varies from session to session. Sometimes, the membranes are extremely tight, but over time, they are becoming more and more responsive, and I can more easily feel the pumping action of cerebrospinal fluid doing its job to keep Logan alive, well, and ready to challenge the world.

As for Logan, he loves CST. Whenever he comes for a session, he jumps right up on the table and is ready to go. His mom told me that because of the chemotherapy, he has lost a lot of hearing and so was delayed in speech development. Once, when Logan's older brother was present, Logan pointed to his brother smiling, then to himself, then to me. He repeated this several times. I think what he was saying to his brother was, "This is cool, man. You ought to try this!"

David Christine has been a hands-on healer for over thirty years and has practiced craniosacral therapy for over twenty years. He is certified as a craniosacral therapist by the Upledger Institute in West Palm Beach Gardens, Florida. An expert in vertigo relief, his technical paper on the subject has been published in the peer-reviewed journal *Alternative Therapies in Health and Medicine*. Craniosacral therapy is helpful for a wide variety of conditions including vertigo, migraines, postconcussion syndrome, asthma, head and neck pain, and many other conditions involving the central nervous system. For more information on craniosacral therapy, visit www.Upledger.com. To learn more about how craniosacral therapy relieves vertigo when all else fails, visit www. UnDizzyMe.com.

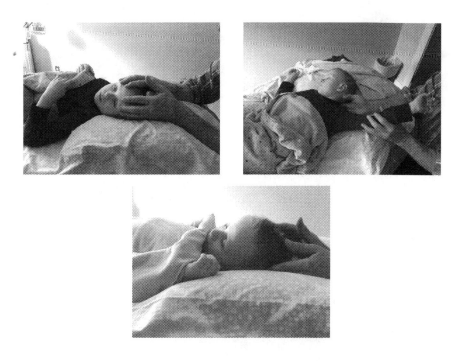

Chapter 15

CHEMOTHERAPY, RADIATION, AND SURGERY OH MY!

Logan started chemotherapy on September 1, 2009. He endured many rounds of various types of toxic chemo to kill his cancer cells. After two relapses, even more chemo was used than in our original protocol that involved six rounds.

He has also been exposed to a lot of radiation. When they took the tumor out of his abdomen, they radiated that spot but also the spot behind his eye where a tumor had metastasized. When he relapsed in the brain, they radiated the spot where the tumor was as well as his whole brain and spine. All that radiation in a little boy who is so young was intense.

Questions constantly swarm our thoughts and invade our hearts. What will the effects of this be on him later in life? Will those toxins create other cancers? What is that chemo and radiation doing to his little organs? We could anguish over those questions for years to come, but instead, we try to repair what damage was done. We use the daily drops of our supplements to try to replenish his body and hopefully reverse some of that damage. We aren't waiting for problems to come up; we're struggling to stay ahead of the game. It is a constant battle watching for the beast in Logan's past, those he valiantly fought for years.

Chapter 16

ESSENTIAL OILS

We also do some essential oils for Logan. For the past couple of years, we have done research on frankincense oil because we had heard how beneficial it was in fighting cancer. Frankincense was one of the oils that the three wise men brought baby Jesus. I tell people that if the wise men brought it to Jesus, that stuff must be good. I believe that the wise men weren't just bringing wealth to Jesus but also medicine.

For over 5,000 years, frankincense has been used to support the immune system, fight infection, and even cure disease. We already know that a big part of keeping Logan in remission involves boosting his immune system. Today, the most common benefits of this oil are many.

- reduces inflammation
- destroys cancer
- increased spiritual awareness
- boosts immunity
- fights infections
- reduces anxiety
- heals skin and reduces acne and scarring

For years, I have rubbed frankincense oil on Logan's feet at night. It is a calming tradition we started, and he actually asks for the oil. Here are some facts about using essential oils. They should be applied to the thinnest part of your skin, so we apply them to our wrists and feet or behind our ears. They can also be applied directly on the area of focus such as the throat for the thyroid, temples for the head, and so on.

Essential oils are unique in that they can pass through the epidermal barrier and enter the bloodstream without causing injury or triggering inflammation or water loss. This is due to their small molecular structure and weight that allows them to penetrate the skin readily. Essential oils are not water soluble; their oil and lipid solubles further facilitate entry through the epidermis. Essential oils are safe and nontoxic; many of them are considered GRAS (generally regarded as safe) by the FDA. The oils can reach the cells in five minutes and peak at twenty minutes.

We found many more beneficial oils that can help on a daily basis whether going through treatments or not. One side effect of chemo is nausea, which peppermint oil can soothe. Citric oils such as grapefruit, orange, and lemon help detoxify the body. This might be useful after treatment or just throughout the year for everyone.

A holistic health coach who utilizes oils can guide you on which ones would best support your needs. A good friend of mine, the owner of Blissful Existence, does just this. Her role as a health coach is to review your health history, and based on your health, wellness, and lifestyle, she offers support through specialized nutritional plans and health remedies. Essential oils increase the benefits of the programs she offers.

She gave me so much information on which oils she felt would be best for Logan. Her passion and excellent training really shine through. She shares her training and knowledge of over a hundred dietary theories and offers daily support to help you become the healthiest version of yourself you can be. What a valuable resource she has been to my family. She can be reached at www.BlissfulExistence.us.

Chapter 17

A Healing Attitude

I have talked a lot about keeping positive thoughts and positive attitudes through our journey and in life in general. It was critical for our day-to-day survival. I believe attitude is everything; it can make or break you. You can and do feed off others' energy. I knew that Logan would feed off my energy, so I always tried to stay upbeat. If I showed him fear, he would feed off that fear. If I were upset, he'd be upset.

No matter what we were dealt, I always tried to project happiness and calmness especially in front of him. I wanted my attitude to provide him comfort, security, and a sense of control when I was struggling with these issues. At times, my faith was pushed to the limits. I had my breakdowns. I had my fears. But controlling them and not letting them control me was of paramount importance. Never showing distress and breakdowns to Logan was crucial. Doctors will tell you that children are resilient mainly because they don't carry all the baggage and fears adults do.

After Logan's major abdominal surgery, we had to wait until he was fully awake before they took all tubes and wires off him to transport him. One such tube was in Logan's side meant for abdominal draining. Before we could transport him to Sloan to continue chemo, they needed to pull that tube out. They used no anesthesia or numbing medicine at all. The tube was sutured in his side, below his ribs and a couple of inches deep. So pulling it out wasn't as easy as one two three.

Logan's Uncle Sal and Aunt Karen were visiting and helping us transition over to Sloan. While they were pulling the tube out, I couldn't bear to watch the process. I told Logan in the most lighthearted voice, "Okay, buddy, we're almost done. This is it. We can go. No more ouchies. It's all done. I promise." All positive words and tones even though inside I was dying. Uncle Sal had a look of horror on his face as they pulled the tube out; if the sight of the removal made a grown man, a cop, a war vet look like that, it must have been awful, but I didn't have the strength to look. Logan's piercing scream told all and reinforced the need for me to help him through his horrors to leave behind this dark place in his life. We really needed to hurry past the pain and focus on getting out of there.

It was just one of the countless times that I had to put on a good persona no matter how my heart was breaking. But even I fed off that energy. Trying to keep things going and to keep things light helped me avoid focusing on the negatives and the desperation of our situation. If I started feeling sorry for Logan and the terrible effects it was having on our family, that wouldn't have changed anything or made them any better; it made me feel worse. So I realized the need for expending all my energies on thinking positive, on building a strong faith that could carry me through.

This is really a life lesson I live with and practice every day. I have always been an upbeat, positive person. It is only when you are pushed to limits and have your faith tested that you realize how important those qualities are.

Chapter 18

Buying Stock in White Out

I had to get used to continually adjusting to many things after we entered the world of cancer; one of many was white out. I use a plain, old calendar date book to mark down appointments and such rather than a fancy phone app. It's part of my OCD when it comes to being and staying organized. I love having it all out in front of me. Notations about gymnastics, mommy-and-me classes, parties, on and on, were quickly replaced with chemo schedules, hospital stays for fevers, and waiting for counts to recover so we could continue treatment.

It wasn't until almost two years later, when Logan was in remission, that we were able to plan parties and trips. Before that, we'd make tentative plans for such but would meet with much disappointment. This was especially difficult for the planner in me; I like to have a schedule and order, but I had to let that go quickly on this journey.

We also missed out on a lot of other things. The most difficult memory denied me happened when my sister gave birth to her first daughter, Payton Mary. I was supposed to be with her at the blessed occasion. Unfortunately, Logan had relapsed and was in treatment in New York when my sister went into labor. Being in treatment is depressing enough, but missing such a beautiful experience added salt to my gaping wound. It was hard to stay positive and not get even more agitated about our situation. I felt like beautiful blessings were going on around us while we sat in a hospital room. Just a little over a year prior to that event, my feet were planted in a hospital with Logan instead of in the sand next to my sister on a beach as she exchanged wedding vows with my brother-in-law. Life was quickly passing by as my little angel fought the beast.

I guess in time we almost got used to that. We had to put Logan and his treatment above everything else. Even though we were sad to miss out on such things, I know I was right where I needed to be—there for Logan and finding his cure. I tried to always remind myself that life wouldn't always be like that. We would overcome and get back to a normal life. Having those positive thoughts for the future carried me through; it got me up in the morning and gave me the strength to keep fighting right beside Logan.

Chapter 19

FRENEMIES

During our journey with Logan, we met many people—oncology parents with whom we shared a deep bond, and a slew of medical people including doctors, nurses, and support staff. We gained friends and of course lost friends. Some friends we'd had since childhood just didn't step up to the plate, while others were e-mailing and texting constantly just to check in or let us know they were thinking of us.

Some friends parted ways with us because they couldn't deal with our constant no-shows for trips or parties. Even when we would get home from the hospital, I was withdrawn. I missed my family being all together. So even when we were in between treatments, I distanced myself from many outside activities. I wanted to be home. I wanted my family together. My emotions were on such a roller-coaster that it wasn't like I was home and happy and that everything was well. I fought depression that would come on when I thought about upcoming treatments, and it didn't disappear when I was home on a break.

Some people didn't understand why I didn't reach out to them more, why I didn't just go out and resume normal activities. Some people questioned why I didn't act like a friend. It's impossible to get people to understand unless they've gone through it themselves. I focused hard on being a hundred percent mom and wife, and that left me drained. It wasn't that I didn't care what was going on in others' lives, but I was emotionally tapped out.

Not everyone is cut out to handle the cancer world and all that comes with it. Even though these were very difficult times, I didn't have a choice. Friends, on the other hand, have choices. I appreciate people who have been in my life, but I realize they don't always have to stay there. It was important for me to surround myself with only a tight, close-knit group of supporters. Life is too short to surround yourself with people who aren't there when you really need them. Of course, friends are there for the good times, but it's when things get dark that you find out who's in your true support group.

We feel very fortunate to have been surrounded by amazing family and friends who got us through everything. Now, they rejoice and celebrate with us as we enjoy Logan's remission.

Chapter 20

CHEMOTHERAPY—
MARRIAGE THERAPY

"For better or for worse, in sickness and in health …" Those were the promises my husband and I made to each other. People getting married say those words, but can they really stand by them?

This is a tougher subject to get in to. Jason and I had what I considered a strong marriage going into this. We had very good communication and similar values, and we were honestly each other's best friend. But this trial pushed our marriage to its limits. We had to deal with such stress, worry, and anger. Even though we shared all our feelings, we definitely dealt with them differently. Many times, we had to suppress our feelings to just go into survival mode and deal with the day-to-day cancer drama. Over time, we built up an animosity toward each other, and we didn't have the time to deal with it because we felt like we were both just trying not to drown.

We reached the point that we couldn't talk without fighting, and we were still dealing with major treatment decisions for Logan. We had a laundry list of disappointments we felt the other was responsible for and hadn't resolved. Our disagreements consisted of one point leading to another before we resolved the first point.

We decided on marriage counseling, and that turned out to be the best thing we could have done. It really helped to have a guided argument or discussion in which the therapist helped us resolve one issue before moving on to the next one. Counseling gave us back respect for one another. I was forced to hear what he was feeling, and he was forced to hear what I was feeling. We both dropped our guards, and our anger started to fade. We started to realize that it wasn't the fault of either of us and that we were dealing with our situation in our own ways.

After several months of therapy, we were back on Team Snyder and tried to make all decisions for Logan together. This was a huge growing point in our lives and our marriage.

Chapter 21

SECURITY FOR TWO

Logan's story would not be complete without giving due acknowledgment to his special blue blanket, which appears in nearly all Logan's hospital pictures; it was attached to him every step of the way. Many children have a special blanket, toy, or binkie they rely on to give them comfort and peace when they are tired or sick, but Logan's blanket went way above and beyond the normal call of duty. His blanket imparted comfort to him when I couldn't; it provided him with a sense of calm when he was in unbearable pain.

He'd push his lips against it and nurse on it. It was a habit he started when he was just a baby. I would nurse him, and man, he loved to nurse. Once he had enough milk, I'd lay him down with this blanket next to his face. He would start to nurse on the blanket and would fall asleep. His attachment to his blanket started way before treatments even began.

We all knew how important his blanket was to him. It wasn't until more recently that I realized how much of an emotional connection I had with it as well. While getting scans in New York in February 2015, the blue blanket was of course along for the ride. Especially now that he is able to undergo MRIs without anesthesia, his blanket helps him through.

Getting scans are always a crazy time; they involve appointment after appointment. We have to meet with nurses, the neuroblastoma team, and the long-term care team and then go for the scans. We would plan lots of fun stuff to do in the city in the evenings during those times; our days and nights were packed.

One time, somehow, amid all the craziness, we lost Logan's blanket. It wasn't until evening when we were relaxing at the Ronald McDonald House that we even noticed it wasn't there. The boys were busy putting together some Lego sets we had bought when Logan asked for his blanket. It was starting to get close to bedtime, and as he grew tired, he wanted it. Jason and I looked at each other and froze. We searched the room everywhere and tried to remember the last time he'd had it. My heart dropped. I called Sloan to see if anyone there had found it. The words cut through me when I heard no one had. At least they agreed to keep an eye out for it.

I couldn't believe it. How could we have possibly left it somewhere? Something that had been with us on our journey for so long was gone. I couldn't sit at the Ronald and just imagine where it was; I had to look for it. I walked the couple of blocks to Sloan to search for it. Jason didn't understand why I was so upset over it; he assumed it was my pregnancy hormones. I'm sure they weren't helping the situation, but it wasn't about that. It was about this immense loss I felt. I knew Logan didn't rely on this blanket at that point as much as he had during treatment, but he still loved it and fell asleep every night snuggling with it.

I tried to remember when we'd had it last. I had this feeling of loss and worry; I was fearful we'd never see it again. What if we'd left it in a cab? Someone would find it and probably throw it out, not understanding all the memories that were attached to this one piece of fabric.

Before getting to Sloan, I stopped at the pizza place where we'd had lunch. I frantically asked the staff, but they acted as if they had no idea what I was talking about. I looked under the tables and in the bathroom. No luck. I continued to Sloan, right to the MRI floor. I knew he'd had it during the MRI; that was the last time I remembered seeing it. I thought we could have left it in the waiting room. When Logan would come out from the hour-and-a-half scan, we'd make such a big deal about his pictures being over and how proud we were that he had lain still that whole time. (It really is an amazing feat for a child his age to be able to do that. Logan never ceases to amaze us.)

The employees checked and double-checked the rooms, but once again, no luck. I went to the floor where Logan had had an EKG. By that time, it was 7:00 or so in the evening, and most everyone had gone home. The once-full waiting room was empty. The usually busy phones were silent. Half the lights were off. The empty room felt eerie, just like I felt. I walked to the room and searched the bed he had lain on for his test, but once again, no luck.

The last chance was the pediatric floor, which I had called earlier. I ran from spot to spot. My heart was beating out of my chest. I clung to the hope I would find it. I ran into the playroom and saw one of the last people still working there. I mentioned how I had just called about my son's blanket. She said, "Oh, I just found it and gave it to the girl out there." I bounded out the door to the reception area before she even finished her sentence. There it was, neatly folded on her desk. The receptionist was picking up the phone to call me. She handed it to me right away. I lost it. I really lost it! I grabbed the blanket and sobbed. I tried to speak, but nothing but tears came out. I could only smile. She said, "Ahh! I'm so happy we found it." She looked very confused about why I had been so upset but was then so happy, but I knew she would never really understand what the three of us had been through. She would never know how just cleaning it was nearly impossible, how I had to sneak the blanket out of his hospital room when he had finally fallen asleep to wash the blood, etc. out of it. Nor would she be able to empathize with the hours of sleep it cost me to make sure it was washed and dried before my little one awoke or just reached out for his blanket's comfort. She would also never comprehend how this tattered piece of cloth made Logan's day bearable. How could she ever understand all that and more?

I clung to that blanket the whole way back to the Ronald McDonald House. I kept thanking God for guiding me to it. I realized it was just a physical thing; I realized the most important thing was having my son, not the blanket, physically with me. But no one would truly understand how his blanket had almost become another child to me. It was always Logan, me, and his blanket through everything. When people came and went for visits, it was always the three of us remaining. When Logan would cry out in pain and no amount of drugs helped, his blanket gave him his only relief.

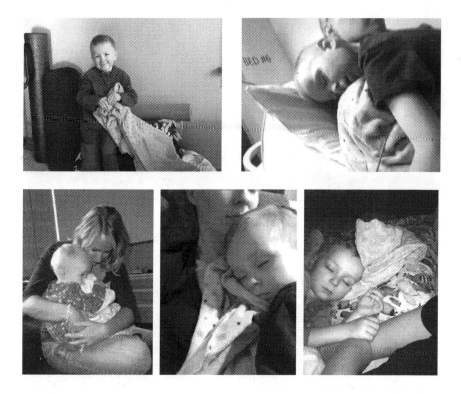

The blanket was important to him, but it was important to me as well. I didn't fully understand how much it had meant to me until we didn't have it. When I handed the blanket to Logan, he took it and just went to playing with the Legos. I had been more upset that it had been missing than he was; he hadn't known his precious binky had been in danger that night. I was and will forever be grateful that God was watching out for us that night.

Chapter 22

A New Enemy in Town

We had to face the long-term side effects from the treatment Logan had received. We were entering a new arena of fearful unknowns. Once he was lucky enough to be in remission for a few years, Logan was passed from his oncology team to a long-term care follow-up team. Its main objective was to track and test him every six months and then eventually annually. Their workup includes blood work, testing urine, and conducting physicals. There are many things to monitor and track.

We were beyond thrilled to have made it to that milestone of prolonged remission, at which point his oncology team felt comfortable passing him along for follow-up care. Unfortunately, the list of late-term effects of chemo and radiation is very long and overwhelming. Here are a couple of personal ones Logan and many children have already encountered.

Hearing Loss from Chemo

Chemo can cause many damaging side effects. Yes, it can be effective in killing cancer cells, but it also kills healthy ones and can wreak havoc on organs and tissue. Many cancer drugs have a good number of side effects—some common, others less common, and some rare. I won't go into the rare column because that's too much, too scary, and usually ends in death.

One of the very common and most likely side effects is hearing loss, but its extent can't be predicted. You enter treatment with the hope that it won't happen, and if it does, that it will be slight. But even with only high-frequency hearing loss, hearing aids could still be needed, as we found out in October 2012.

Logan had several hearing tests. They were thinking that though he had suffered some high-frequency hearing loss, it wasn't enough for him to get hearing aids. But as he got older and became more capable of completing the tests with more accuracy, it was evident he needed them. His speech was also affected because of his inability to hear many sounds. We of course were disappointed that his once-perfect hearing had been damaged by the drugs they had given him, but the alternative, of course, was so much worse. We took that news in stride and were happy to see the difference when he got hearing aids. A new world opened before him. Unfortunately, our Rife machine doesn't have a setting to repair hearing loss; once those delicate hairs are damaged, they cannot grow back or be repaired. Logan has adjusted to his hearing loss as children who need glasses adjust to them. Below is a picture of Logan getting his hearing aid molds made.

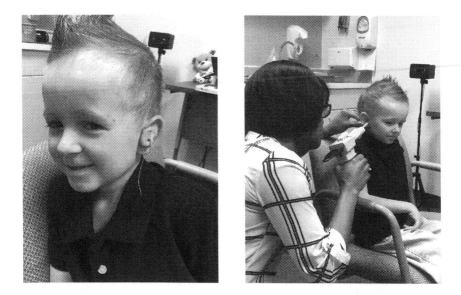

Could the hearing loss have been prevented? According to our oncologists, no. They had given Logan Cisplatin and hoped it wouldn't affect his hearing too much. That is not true. In studies of some rats,

Cisplatin-induced ototoxicity was avoided by the use of vitamins E, B and C, and L-carnitine. In those studies, all rats were given Cisplatin. Some of them were also given vitamins B, E, C or L-carnitine preceding the Cisplatin. ABR (auditory brainstem response) tests and distortion product otoacoustic emissions were recorded on the rats before and seventy-two hours after the Cisplatin was administered. Guess what? Significant differences were seen.

The result was that vitamins B, E, and C and L-carnitine appear to reduce Cisplatin-induced ototoxicity in the rats. Of course, no such studies have been done on humans. I wish I had found this information before so we could have tried it. It is amazing how many studies they do and protocols they create not ever knowing the lasting effects on children. But they continue in hopes they will cure cancer and keep children in remission.

When we asked if we could try natural supplements to help, they discouraged us. Our medical doctors did not want us doing any natural supplements for fear they would interfere with the chemo. I agree that some supplements can interfere with chemo, but why not try something as harmless as vitamins E, B, C, and L-carnitine if it means it could save children's hearing? My objective now is to get that information out there for others.

Growth Hormone Deficiency

Monitoring children's height and weight is a huge part of what the long-term care team focuses on. Since Logan had had radiation to his abdomen, spine, and brain, his chances were greater for his growth to be stunted. Radiation basically stops or slows the growth of whatever it hits, so we were afraid Logan would be affected in the long term.

His height and weight are checked each visit. He doesn't have to be on a specific spot on the growth curve; he just has to show improvement. If he starts to plateau, they test him for growth-hormone deficiency. If he is deficient, insurance will cover growth-hormone treatment; he will receive daily shots of a synthetic version of normal growth hormones produced by the pituitary gland in the brain. Of course, with anything, there are side effects. This type of testing and intervention is every parent's decision. Our long-term care team didn't push the hormones either way. They provide the testing and information and put the ball in our court. Another major, life-changing decision we have to make as parents.

Once again, we turned to our naturalist. She gave us several supplements to stimulate the pituitary gland and thyroid to produce hormones. We're also giving Logan an all-natural growth hormone. Will they work? Only time will tell, but there's no guarantee even with the synthetic growth hormones. No one knows how tall or big Logan would have been, but figuring that out is not important. We based our decision on the fact that the daily shots would have side effects, one of which could be leukemia. Short, tall, medium, or small, he'll be loved and happy. We will ultimately instill in him how lucky he is to be here no matter his size.

Developmental Delays

Because of the treatments and especially the full-brain radiation, Logan has had developmental delays. Radiation basically stunts the growth of what it hits. This will just be something we'll have to work on and watch. He did have speech delays due to needing hearing aids. He also was not ready to begin kindergarten until he turned six. As he continues through the school system, they are closely monitoring him and pulling him out for whatever extra help he needs.

Dermatologist Checks

Because of the several spots Logan had had radiated, we must keep a close eye on his skin. Annually checks with the dermatologist ensure that there is no damage or growth from the radiation exposure.

Dental Issues

One more side effect of chemotherapy is damage to the teeth, both baby teeth and the dormant adult teeth. Logan has already had a tooth pulled and several cavities filled, and his teeth are a bit discolored. We'll have to wait until more adult teeth come in to see what effects it's had on them.

A Mother's Worry

This particular long-term side effect affects me more so than it does Logan. Once your child has been diagnosed with cancer, you know your life will never be the same, but it might be even years later when you realize how much your life has truly changed. What is really taken from a mother is her sanity, peace, and comfort.

You always hear of a mother's worry, but cancer in a child can put that in overdrive. After your child is diagnosed with cancer, nothing seems little anymore. Each ache or pain Logan has sends my mind directly into a cancer spin. He will sometimes say his belly hurts, and I immediately think he has a tumor in his abdomen. If he rubs his head, I think he has a brain tumor once again. So how exactly can I deal with these somewhat irrational scenarios? I say somewhat irrational because they are totally understandable when you've seen what we've seen. At one time, he was rubbing his head due to a brain tumor. Of course, cancer could return at any time, without warning and without prejudice; that's the nature of the beast.

I spoke with Logan's doctors to find out how I could deal with my fear better. Unfortunately, they had no real answers. There is no way to rule out cancer without doing scans. They might have a fever with it, but they might not. They might be lethargic from it, but they might not.

So knowing his cancer could return, how can we handle our fears of that? What can we do? It will be a daily struggle, something I have to work on as a mom. I have to maintain faith that we are doing all we can to make his body strong enough to fight this enemy. I also have to deal with the fact that kids have normal pains and aches.

Our routine scans help calm my fears. I hate to use them as a security blanket, but that's what they are. They give us confidence and reassurance that his inside looks as good as his outside does. I hate going through the stress of scans and putting Logan through the hospital scene, but the peace they offer is priceless.

Post-Traumatic Stress Disorder (PTSD)

PTSD is usually associated with trauma victims such as Logan, war veterans, and residents of communities who have suffered through disasters. This disorder extends to the parents of trauma victims. Unless you have been through a traumatic experience, this may be hard to understand. It can come over you in an instant for numerous reasons. Jason and I noticed that we would go into periods of depression randomly. It could be something as simple as reading a past Caring Bridge entry that would trigger it. It would almost bring us back to that exact moment in history.

One particular day, Jason came home from work and was in a miserable mood. I figured it had been just a bad day at work, so I left him alone. But he told me he had gotten a fax from Sloan of Logan's medical chart. We had needed it so we could get it to our new pediatrician. He said that he had an overwhelming sickness as he read through the chart and saw the scans, reports, and treatments all listed in one neat little package—page after page of information detailing Logan's treatments. It took us back to that time and triggered all those fears and negative emotions we once had.

Such triggers would get us into a funk or depression we couldn't just snap out of. Neither of us understood it. How could we be so upset about something that had been over for years? Logan was home and doing fabulously, and we had no reason to get down. All we had to do was watch him thrive; all was good. But at random times, events trigger memories of that time when things weren't awesome at all. It can take some time, but we eventually move past it and resume our normal life. We soon recognized when one or the other was feeling this, and we have supported each other.

I wondered about writing this book because I knew that would require me to relive the journey. I'd have to read my entries I had typed in dark hospital rooms. The only sounds were beeping machines, clicking computer keys, and sobs of a broken mother. I didn't want to look back; I wanted to keep facing forward and push away the fears and disappointments I once had.

We realize that part of our lives will never go away. Some days, we will feel their impact, but mostly, they're left in the past. Allowing yourself to grieve for a time is a good release. Things weren't always unicorns and butterflies. It's okay to not want to relive all those memories; releasing that energy and moving on is important. Jason and I understand that. We occasionally get into bad moods, but we support one another. It is just one of those things that unless you have been through it, you just don't get it.

Chapter 23

CARING BRIDGE
SITE A GODSEND

When Logan was first diagnosed, we relied on close family to pass on Logan's updates. Everyone was wondering what was happening, how he was doing, and what our plans were.

Soon after Logan's diagnosis, my sister Brandy told me about the Caring Bridge website. She created an account for Logan, and within days, I was updating everyone on his progress. Writing on this site was therapeutic just as writing this book was. Jotting down the day's events gave me a sense of control when I felt I had none; I was putting it all out there so we could get prayers, and that was a wonderful comfort. I also felt it would be a great journal for Logan to have when he grew up. Though he'll never remember all that had happened, I'll never forget any of it. Here's the first journal entry I made while in the PICU at CHOP.

Thursday, August 27, 2009 4:34 p.m.

Thank you all for your caring words of support. We are taking it one day at a time. Brandy told me about this website, and I think it is a great way for us to keep all of you in the loop on how Logan is doing.

We moved from Lehigh Valley Cedar Crest to CHOP (Children's Hospital of Philadelphia) today. We should be meeting with the oncologist soon. Logan is doing okay and looking forward to starting treatment so he can feel better fast.

I remember sitting in a tiny playroom just a couple of doors down from Logan's PICU room. The PICU floor was full of fear and beeping machines and stress but under an eerie quiet. I was trying to log on; I wanted to get the word out so prayers could start coming. Logan needed them, I needed them, and our family needed them.

I saw something that will stay with me until the day I die. In one of the rooms was a boy probably around ten. He had a thick and dark full head of hair. He was lying unconscious. I had no idea what had brought him there. All of a sudden, lights and alarms outside his room started going off. The floor changed from a quiet, peaceful place to an almost chaotic area full of nurses and doctors who were buzzing in and out of his room, closely watching the monitors, trying everything to save him. I watched in pure fear of what was happening. Logan was sleeping peacefully, so my full attention was drawn to this horrible situation.

In the end, the doctors' and nurses' efforts had failed. I saw that they had realized he had passed. Everything stopped. I had to watch family come in and out of the room to say their good-byes. I saw the little boy's big brother say good-bye. He ended up leaving the room with his hands covering his eyes. He was crying uncontrollably.

It was a night I will never forget. It was also a night that brought even more fear into our situation. I cried myself to sleep for that little boy and for my little angel. I couldn't believe what had happened to my world. That was my first night in a PICU, and I had to witness that. No hope. No peace. As if my introduction into the world of cancer wasn't hard enough. That seemed more than I could bear. But it happened. It stayed with me, and it always will. I realized at that moment that no matter how awful my situation seemed, someone always had it worse, so I should be thankful my son was sleeping peacefully.

Caring Bridge is a wonderful website that help people update the situation when they are dealing with medical crises. It is free and easy to set up. It feels so good to know I can reach many people who love Logan and follow his story faithfully. It also provides an avenue for comfort and support from all the readers who can respond and offer closeness even from afar.

Caring Bridge is also a great resource for getting information and making contacts. When I was interested in going toward a more vegetarian/vegan diet for our family, I posted a message in the hopes of getting some recipes. A woman I used to know instantly contacted me with a resource. Once we were connected, she and her husband shared so much information and valuable recipes. It was just what we needed at that time to make such a change in our lifestyle and diet.

Although Caring Bridge was factual, I rarely updated how I was doing. I avoided the really negative nature of the situation because I felt I needed to keep it together and stay positive for Logan. I knew he was feeding off my energy, so I tried to stay as upbeat as possible. That doesn't mean I didn't have breakdowns or didn't seek release from my anger through tears—just not in front of him and never on Caring Bridge. I didn't let people into what it was really like being away from home and my other son and husband; that would have been too much. I felt the point of Caring Bridge was to get prayers from our friends and family because I believe in the power of prayer. Life in the hospital wasn't always as portrayed in my journal entries; it wasn't always the pretty, positive, pink picture I painted. What was accurate was how Logan was always a trooper and was handling everything in an amazing way. His strength was what got me through.

Chapter 24

BIG BROTHER JEFFREY AND OUR SUPPORT GROUP

How can you be a good mom to two boys when one has so many needs? You always feel deficient. I missed so much time with Jeffrey. My fear was that he would have security issues with a mom and brother always missing and a dad who had to work to provide for us. Jeffrey once told someone that his mommy and brother lived in New York and his daddy worked. I still feel guilt and regret for not having been there for Jeffrey. He didn't have cancer, but he still needed his mom.

Lucky for us, we have an amazing family support system. Both my parents and Jason's parents live within ten minutes of us. They not only stepped up to the plate, they went above and beyond anything I could have imagined. They took amazing care of Jeffrey while we were away, and they made sure he was part of their visits to see us. It was critical for Jeffrey and Logan to be together like brothers should be even if it wasn't in the most favorable and fun settings.

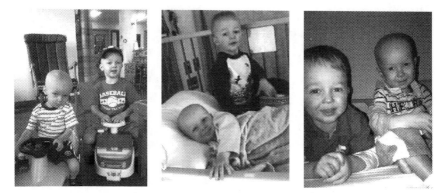

Our parents' tireless efforts included driving us to appointments and making meals for us when we were at the hospital and at home. They helped us out financially as well. In every aspect, they held us up and helped us bear our burdens. Without that support, we would not be where we are today. For them, this experience was like a double whammy. They had to watch not only their grandson but also their son and daughter go through this trial.

Logan's aunts and uncles also helped out any way they could. Logan's Aunt Karen would make special food and drive it into the city; that was always a wonderful break from the hospital food and takeout.

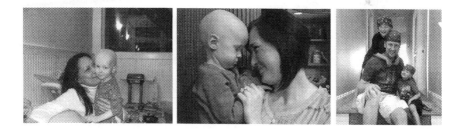

Family and friends sent constant e-mails, texts, and phone calls, and that meant the world to me. It gave me a release; I could open up to them, cry, and ask their advice. It all helped get me through that time away from home. Below are pictures of our team, our biggest supporters with whose help we made it through.

I will never be able to get back the time lost with Jeffrey. The guilt I feel for not having been there daily stays with me. Yes, I know Logan needed me. Yes, I know his life-threatening demands were most pressing. But Jeffrey was still my son who deserved to have his mom by his side. He deserved to have me taking him to school and doing crafts with him. My only hope is that when Jeffrey is older, he will understand why I was missing so much and was so protective of Logan. I want him to understand I sometimes lost my patience over little things because I was dying from stress.

I hope he will someday understand all the times I tried to protect Logan from further injuries when they wrestled with each other. Hopefully, he will understand why I rushed to Logan's aid for fear of his port being damaged. I wanted to protect him from as much pain as I could since I couldn't seem to protect him from cancer. At times, it made it seem I was siding with Logan and pushing Jeffrey aside. At times, I did. I've spent years trying to make up for it. I hope he knows I love him just as much as I do Logan. I hope he realizes I didn't think I had much time left with Logan.

Just as our family and friends came to our rescue, so did our community. As soon as Logan's diagnosis was made public, we had several people in our community express their desire to help us. They organized fundraisers for our medical and travel expenses and to raise awareness of pediatric cancer. We had several benefits including a dodgeball tournament at a school and buffets at restaurants. My nieces Arielle and Alyssa performed in a benefit their dance school put on. I can't describe the financial burden that made Logan's situation that much worse. Jason had to miss a lot of work in the first couple of weeks, and even when he went back to work, his head wasn't in it but on Logan and me. Being a self-employed contractor, he wanted and needed to generate work, but he couldn't get his mind off where his son was.

The financial help we received helped with our travel expenses and treatment co-pays and helped us focus on getting Logan better. As the years went on, people still wanted to do benefits in honor of Logan. So we donated a lot of money to pediatric cancer research at Sloan Kettering. We hope that less-toxic treatments will be developed. We want to aid in discovering therapies that are effective against cancer without bad side effects such as hearing loss and growth issues.

Chapter 25

ANGEL ORGANIZATIONS

Michael's Way

One amazing organization we came in contact with is Michael's Way. Its mission is to improve the lives of children who have cancer and support their parents financially. Michael's Way was founded in 2002 by Chris McElwee, in memory of his brother, Michael, who lost his battle with leukemia at age twenty-five.

Chris was working when he became inspired with an idea. He met a man who had lost his house shortly after his son had been diagnosed with leukemia. It was then that Chris researched how many organizations supported families affected by cancer with their nonmedical bills. Nonmedical, out-of-pocket expenses associated with providing treatment for cancer average 38 percent of a family's gross annual income. However, there are very few charities in the Philadelphia area that reimburse nonmedical expenses, and the maximum amount paid to families is often very low. Michael's Way was founded to fill this need.

Since its inception, Michael's Way has raised more than $6 million to lessen the financial hardships of hundreds of families whose children are suffering from cancer. A hundred percent of money raised as well as private donations and grants from foundations goes directly to the families, not to overhead. They try to ease the financial burden so families can concentrate on the real battle—saving their children's lives.

We didn't come in contact with this organization until a few years into treatment. My sister Brandy was searching for ways to help Logan and other children and discovered Michael's Way. Now she is on the board and does a lot of work advocating for the organization. When they heard about Logan, they asked us to be a part of a campaign to raise pediatric cancer awareness. Logan did a photo shoot with Kevin Kolb, then quarterback of the Philadelphia Eagles. It is great when athletes take time out of their busy schedules to bring awareness to pediatric cancer. The logo for the campaign was "Heros come in all sizes," and that couldn't be more true. Below is the picture of the campaign they ran with him. It was a very fun thing for us to do, and we had hoped would bring attention and raise awareness.

You can read more about this organization and learn how to donate by going to www. michaelsway.com.

Make-A-Wish

We were also fortunate enough to be given an amazing trip during our darkest time. Jason and I were approached by our local hospital's health coordinator who insisted we apply for a wish through Make-A-Wish. At first, I couldn't imagine trying to plan a major trip in between treatments. I wanted to make sure he would be feeling up to it and enjoy every moment. But at the time, it was important that we made as many wonderful memories as we could, not just focus on medical stuff. When you aren't sure your son has a future, a trip to the happiest place on earth, Disney World, gets moved up on your priority list, your bucket list. It is disgusting to think children need a bucket list, but the sad reality is that many do.

So we set the trip up for what we thought would be a break in his treatment and when he would be feeling the best. It was one of the most amazing experiences in all our lives. We stayed at Give Kids the World, which is only for Make-A-Wish recipients; everyone staying there was going through some sort of medical crisis. It is a community that shares the bonds of dealing with sick children.

Give Kids the World offers so many fun activities for the kids including unlimited ice cream and carousel rides, pretty much what every kid wants. We were also given VIP treatment while in the parks with passes that allowed no waits on any rides, extra money for meals, and even a lounge to rest in and take a break from the heat for all Make-A-Wish children. All these added perks made us feel like royalty. It took our minds off worrying about cancer and treatments; all we worried about was having the boys lead us by reading the maps. We cherished each of Logan's laughs and smiles. It was a trip we couldn't have afforded at the time, so to have had it all provided for us was amazing.

This is another organization we donate to and try to raise awareness about. We want to give back what we had received so many years ago in our time of need. Even when my grandfather Domer passed away, in lieu of flowers, we asked people to donate to Make-A-Wish. Instances like that make you feel you are helping give other children the joy you experienced.

Ronald McDonald House

While receiving treatment at Sloan, we were lucky enough to be able to stay at the Ronald McDonald House. Up until diagnosis, I knew of Ronald McDonald only as the guy from the McDonalds restaurant. I had no idea the housing they have set up for kids and their families going through treatment. It was a home away from home. They go above and beyond to make you feel comfortable and to take your mind off your daily struggles. When you come back from a long day at the hospital, almost every night, meals are prepared for you by generous restaurants who donate the meal and serve it. If food isn't provided one night, there are several huge kitchens in which you can prepare your own home-cooked food.

There is also a fabulous playroom where kids can go to feel like kids again after their long and tedious days. I can't even tell you the amazing networking you find. You find other parents who can answer questions, share experiences, or just listen to you vent. All such parents share an unimaginable bond. And the kids get to play with other kids who have ports, loss of hair, and so on, so their troubles seem more normal, and no one feels different.

Chapter 26

GIVING BACK

There are so many wonderful ways to give back. Donating money or time to any of the angel organizations I mentioned in chapter 25 is wonderful. You can also donate a part of you. Until our own personal experience, we were oblivious to cancer, chemo, radiation, and all that went along with keeping Logan alive.

One thing that did keep him alive throughout our entire journey was the donated blood products Logan so desperately received. He needed blood and platelets so many times that I lost count. However, something I never lost count of was the gratitude and relief I felt knowing it was there. It would pump his little body up so he could continue to fight this nasty beast; it gave his little body energy as well as the strength to keep going. Without those precious bags of blood and platelets, Logan would have certainly died. Now, because of all those generous donors and our team of doctors, Logan is a healthy and happy seven-year-old. I cannot thank enough the people who take time out to donate, which literally saves lives, including my son.

Every year, we organize a blood drive in honor of Logan. We feel it is just one way we can give back to such a wonderful cause. Over the years, the attendance has grown, and we hope to continue to do it every year. Raising awareness about the need for blood donations and putting a face on a recipient who was saved by them is our goal. The donated blood products and platelets help cancer patients and others who need blood due to accidents or surgeries. People of all ages benefit from these blood products. The blood banks usually have critically low supplies, so they are always in need of generous donors. It's a cause dear to my heart, and I will continue to work to pump those blood banks back up.

Chapter 27

A Spiritual Look

"Faith is the substance of things hoped for, the evidence of things not seen"; Hebrews 11:1 quickly became our anchor in these times of trial and tribulation. There were so many times when I questioned why this had happened to us. Why Logan? Why do some kids respond to treatment but others die? Why do kids even get cancer? Why have I read other Caring Bridge blogs about parents watching their children suffer in pain from cancer taking over their little bodies and holding them as they take their last breaths? To even think these parents were there when their babies took their first breaths and when they took their last is incomprehensible.

All I do know is that we live in an evil world. Evil is permitted, but sometimes miracles do happen. I believe evil is permitted as tests and lessons for us. It may not seem fair, and it isn't. Nothing is right about anything in the cancer world, but with all the bad, I have also seen the good. I've witnessed blessings, triumphs, and miracles, including Logan. The lessons I learned from Logan's journey I carry with me every day. I am a better person, wife, friend, and mom because of everything I have witnessed and gone through. Jason is a better husband and father also because of his experience.

I do believe that one day there will be no sickness, there will be no evil. We will carry the lessons we learn in this world into the next. These lessons, as hard as they are, will give us empathy and compassion we may not have had or truly understood before our experience. I am confident that God is a loving God and has a plan.

Even though we live in an evil world where these injustices are permitted, there are comforting reassurances based on our deep faith in God. These manifest themselves in many different ways. I have been consoled many times by what appeared to be messages from God. One such experience was when we received the news that Logan was HAMA positive. This blood test basically indicated that Logan's body couldn't receive the 3F8 medicine at that time. We were trying to get in as many rounds of the 3F8 as he could, thinking it would teach his body to fight the cancer on its own. When you are not getting the 3F8, you worry that the cancer will start to grow again. Waiting for the HAMA to become negative so you can resume treatment again is very stressful.

The morning we received the news, I was in our bathroom getting ready for the day. I was thinking of all the possibilities and worry that come from not receiving any treatment. I instantly stopped myself from letting my mind wonder and just said, "It is fine. This is what Logan's body needs, and he is going to be fine." At that moment, the sun popped out from behind a cloud and the sunlight just poured into our bathroom. It was so incredibly bright that my eyes shut. I felt the warmth. Time stood still. I thought it was God's way of telling me I was right, a confirmation of what I had just said. It gave me a great amount of peace that morning and is a memory I carry with me.

Another such experience involved a rainbow. Even years before our journey with Logan, the rainbow has had a great impact on Jason and me. At our wedding reception, a double rainbow filled the sky and blessed our special day and union. We got some amazing pictures and it was a huge highlight from that day.

The rainbow was a sign from God after the flood as a promise to the world. I believe rainbows are beautiful encouragements from God. We also saw a gorgeous rainbow the first time we brought Logan home from the hospital after he had endured his first round of chemo. As we were unpacking the car, we looked up in amazement and enjoyed its splendor. We stared in awe at the heavens that day with hope in our hearts for God's mercy. A rainbow appeared the day we brought our fourth baby Mia home from the hospital; another precious time a rainbow shared our blessed day.

I truly believe God shows mercy and can send us messages even through others. One particular story my mother-in-law shared was something she experienced when Logan was first diagnosed. She told me this story years later, and it gave me chills. This is the actual entry she wrote in her journal after it happened.

I need to start documenting all the God "things" I am experiencing. Since Logan got sick on August 23, things had moved quickly. On Tuesday, August 25, Logan had a biopsy in the morning to determine a diagnosis. That morning, I had an appointment at 8:30 a.m. with my gynecologist. I kept my appointment reluctantly! (Jeff insisted I go since it was on our way to the hospital.) That morning, I was so distraught. The office was an hour behind, and sitting and waiting while I could have been at the hospital was more than I could take. I cried in the waiting room, cried in the examination room, and cried in front of Dr. Lionetti.

After paying at the front desk and preparing to leave the waiting area, I saw a woman on the other side of the room rise and start toward me as she was looking straight at me. I turned from her not knowing who she was and started out the door into the hallway by the elevators—she followed me, and I felt her presence and turned around and found her facing me. She embraced me and whispered in my ear, "He is going to be alright." I thought, how did she know what was going on? I assumed she had had a conversation with Jeff while I was in the examination room. I immediately asked Jeff as we were walking out of the building, "Who was that woman?" He said he did not know her but thought I did. I asked him if he talked to her while I was in with the doctor, and he said no.

I remembered this was the woman who had been standing at the front desk window a few feet from me checking in with the receptionist. I had already been waiting a considerable time and had gone back up to the window to see how much longer till I could see the doctor. I was already panicking about not being at the hospital and was thinking of leaving. I remember her presence struck me first and then her blouse caught my eye—it was white, white with some lace and open sleeves. Why I remember this I do not know. I gave her no more thought.

I believe that I was touched by an angel that morning!

Another powerful experience came from my husband Jason. Here is his account of how God reached out to him in a desperate time of need.

Our week began Monday morning at 5 a.m. when we were on our way to New York City to start a round of high-dose 3F8. We arrived and went through the regular routine of getting Logan hooked up to the IVs, blood work, and waiting to get the experimental antibody treatment.

It was so hard to watch my son scream in pain, looking at my wife with tears in her eyes, and holding him, saying it was almost over. So day one is over and four more to go. I stayed with them that night and drove home in the morning to go to work and to spend some time with our other son, Jeffrey, for the rest of the week.

On day 3 of treatment, Logan was not doing well. He would not eat or drink and was so drugged up and miserable. He just lay in his stroller as if he were in a coma. It was so hard to talk to Ashleigh on the phone every night, listening to her cry as she told me how much pain he was in.

On the third night, after treatment, I broke down and gave up on God. I hung up the phone with my wife and threw the phone across the yard, yelling, "God, you coward! Why not me? How can you do this to my baby boy? He is innocent, and you have no compassion for my son!"

I fell in the yard and started to cry. I picked my head up and looked into the deep grass where I saw my cell phone light up, alerting me I had a text message. I slowly picked myself up and walked over to the phone. It was a message from my wife. It was a video of Logan getting out of his stroller and running around the playroom. I must have played it ten times before I called Ashleigh and asked her, "What is going on?"

She said, "Jason, you would not have believed me, so I had to send you a video. Logan went from miserable in his stroller to jumping out of it and then ran to play with the other kids. He starting eating the food I had sitting in front of him." My wife started to cry and said, "It is a miracle!"

I told her that everything was going to be ok, that I would see them tomorrow, and that I loved them very much. I hung up, looked up to the sky, and said, "Lord, I am sorry I gave up on you. Thank you for not giving up on me."

Whether it is a beautiful rainbow, a perfectly planned ray of sun, a text message, or an actual person saying just the right thing, I believe these are all encouragements from God. They are his way of showing us he is with us, he is watching us, he is carrying us through.

Chapter 28

A CLEAN PANTRY

I am sure many parents reading this change in diet are laughing at the idea of their children eating so healthy. I hear so many moms say they can't get their children to eat anything healthy. It can be a challenge; I deal with resistance. Logan feels better on healthy foods, but Jeffrey, who has not been held to as strict a regimen, tends to resist at times. I prepare the same foods for them with a few exceptions since I know it is best for everyone.

Here are some tips that might help. Start off healthy right from the beginning. If your children haven't had pizza, ice cream, and candy, they don't know any better. I really never gave them candy, soda, or fast foods. However, now that I understand the benefits of whole foods better, I started Hope off eating just what they ate. She eats hard-boiled eggs, chickpeas, and cucumbers for lunch. That is what I have always put before her, so she knows nothing else. Of course, if she sees something else, she will want it. So I try to offer her only healthy choices and make sure to eat the same.

Give fruit as a treat. It is sweet and delicious and can even be made into ice cream, smoothies, or popsicles. This is a great way to sneak healthy foods such as spinach or flaxseed into their treats. I blend frozen bananas and blueberries to make homemade ice cream. Adding healthy, whole foods stays hidden behind the delicious fruit. They get a kick out of making it, so it's a fun activity as well. Below is a picture of Logan making our homemade popsicles. He enjoys making them, and I enjoy sneaking in all that goodness.

Eating healthy can roll right into holiday traditions. One holiday my children look forward to is Easter. They love going on egg hunts and finding their Easter baskets, which contain not candy but toys, fun snacks, puzzles, bunny bubbles, coloring books, coins, and so on. They have an awesome time and are so excited to see what they get.

Easter can be just as exciting without chocolate and processed sugar. If this idea doesn't appeal to you, add just one or two of their favorite candy items but keep the majority of their baskets filled with fun items. Below are pictures of their Easter baskets and a fun fruit creation I made. It may not be perfect, but the kids get a kick out of it. There are so many creative ideas online.

For birthdays, I made several fun fruit creations to take the place of the typical, traditional, food-dyed birthday cakes. I was concerned that they would be disappointed when I began to switch from the typical cake, but I was pleasantly surprised to see how excited they were to see their favorite fruit appear in such a dynamic way.

The above picture was taken on Logan's fourth birthday; I made a "cake" entirely of fruit. The look on his face says it all. He was so excited and thought it looked so cool. He loved picking off the fruit, and I loved knowing he was enjoying his birthday without all the unhealthy treats.

This picture was taken on Logan's fifth birthday. I made a chocolate cake, but instead of icing it, I decorated it with fruit. So kids got a small slice of the cake with fruit. I also made individual fruit cups. All were a hit with the kids. I am sure the parents were thankful their kids wouldn't be crashing later from the sugar high.

This picture was taken on Jeffrey's sixth birthday. His birthday falls right around Thanksgiving, so I made his cake following the turkey theme. The turkey tail was individual wooden spears of fruit kabobs. The children pulled each spear out and devoured the fruit.

These last fruit arrangements were some I did for a family barbeque. These are just some creative ideas you can make for celebrations that are still delicious and fun but minus all the harmful ingredients. Going online can help you find some creative and healthy ideas for celebrating any events.

If it isn't in your pantry, your children can't eat it. If I have candy, cookies, or unhealthy snacks, my children are tempted to indulge in them. Keeping such food out of our pantry has helped us all stay on track, especially when they help themselves to my pantry for a snack. They look up and down the shelves and eventually settle on whatever I have. It's either that or go hungry. The meals are so important, but so are snacks during the day.

Those are just a few of the successful ideas I've learned. Even if kids don't have cancer, they can benefit from eating as if they did. No one needs processed sugar; it doesn't help them to grow up healthy and strong.

Chapter 29

A Crystal Ball

No one knows what the future holds. I still think of people who have lost perfectly healthy children in car accidents or other unforeseen situations. They never saw it coming. Life is so fragile.

We haven't talked to the boys yet about the severity of Logan's diagnosis. We don't feel they're mature enough to understand. How can I explain to them why kids get cancer and some even die? I don't want them to fear cancer or worry about it coming back. I plan to keep them in their kid bubbles as long as I can. When they are older, we will address all we have been through as a family.

Right now we explain to Logan why we do his drops and his machine and all that goes with it. We simply tell him it will keep him healthy and out of the hospital. Logan has begun to ask all sorts of questions regarding the bump on his head (his Ommaya port) and the huge scar on his abdomen. He was a little emotional when talking about his hearing aids. We continue to answer his questions as they come, not feeling the need to get into cancer cells and tumors and all that.

If Logan had been older while undergoing treatment, this all would be different I'm sure. I want them to keep their innocence as long as possible. Kids should worry about which trees they can climb and how long they can hold their breath underwater. They shouldn't be worrying about if their cancer is going to come back and make them sick again.

I don't know what Logan's or my futures hold, but I know we can improve our health and lives by watching what we eat and how we take care of ourselves. Above all, God is watching over us. We might not understand the plan he has for us. We might not want to think of bad things happening because we can't imagine a life that way. In the end, I do know there is a purpose. I like to think that mine is to share with people the incredible information I have learned over the past couple of years. We have given our son more time and better health by making these changes. Every day I look at him, I see a miracle.

Logan went from relapsing twice to a four-and-a-half-year run in remission to date. He now attends kindergarten and plays t-ball and soccer. They will continue to scan Logan every six months for the next couple of years. Then he will move to annually and eventually never. He is fortunate that his scans now consist of only blood work, urine analysis, and MRIs of the brain and spine. We feel great about the fact that he no longer needs CT scans due to the radiation exposure. Our doctors look at Logan in awe. One doctor in particular tells us that Logan really had them worried for a while. They think it is just fabulous that he is doing so well, and so do we.

While Logan's experiences were a nightmare for all of us, some positives have come from it. I no longer sweating the small stuff in my daily trials and struggles. I appreciate the little things; that helps me never take a day for granted. I am by no means a perfect mom, but this perspective helps keep me calmer during the day because haunting memories still hold their place in the back of my mind. Being thankful every day, being content with what life brings is a gift many people don't have. I have that, and I feel eternally blessed for it.

Logan is just now rebounding, growing, evolving, and finally feeling comfortable in his own skin. At this point, Logan has been in remission for four and a half wonderful years. As we sang in church on this past Easter Sunday rejoicing in Jesus' resurrection, the children all paraded around the pews with crosses and streamers. Logan had the biggest smile on his face as he proudly waved the cross. Anyone who was acquainted with Logan knew that this was a huge milestone for him. He used to be so shy, hiding behind me, not participating, staring at the floor, and making very little eye contact. He never felt comfortable around new people or more than a handful of people or having the attention on him. For most of his short existence, he was either poked or prodded by medical staff. He spent so much of his time in pain and feeling sick instead of playing and interacting with others. So it always took him time to warm up to someone or to be the center of attention.

His second birthday celebration is a perfect example. Since he had brain surgery on his birthday, we had to delay the festivities until weeks later. He was still feeling very poorly, and he hid behind his blue blanket as we carried him around. There were too many people there for his comfort level even though they were all so anxious to help him celebrate getting though such a difficult surgery.

As I watched him that Sunday in all his glory, I teared up. I became so overwhelmed, and it wasn't due to hormones though I was pregnant with our fourth child. I tried to push the tears away because I didn't want anyone to think anything was wrong. Nothing was wrong. Everything was right. It was an amazing blessing to see Logan so healthy and happy; cancer had stolen so much from him and the rest of us. I can't explain how it feels to know your son is a miracle. God gave me a miracle! I may have experienced some of the darkest lows with Logan, but now, I am able to experience the mountain highs. I have gained so much from Logan and his journey over the years. Hopefully, I have been able to impart just a small part of my heart's sentiments to you.

Chapter 30

MOVING FORWARD

We will continue to do what we are doing for Logan and our family. We know we are promoting a healthier lifestyle everyone should have whether he or she has cancer or not. We should all be more disciplined by eating better and taking care of ourselves.

We do have our "cheat" times. We do go out to eat with Logan, and he goes off his diet a bit. We do allow him some treats here and there. Luckily, he steers clear of most sugary treats because he knows they will make his tummy hurt; his body is not accustomed to sugar and processed food. I hope that when he is older, he will be so used to these good food decisions that he will always choose this healthier path. His body has already adjusted to this better state, and he definitely feels it when he goes off the path.

Don't wait for a cancer diagnosis to make these health changes. If you or someone you know has been diagnosed with cancer, take the several steps I have suggested. I cannot say to not try toxic treatments considering we used them to get rid of Logan's cancer. What I can say is that it was only a quick fix in his case. It is what got him in remission, but it did not keep him there. We know several people who refused to take chemo and beat their cancer with an all-natural approach. I would try anything and everything under the sun to get healthy. Here are some easy steps to help you get started:

1. If diagnosed with cancer, listen to the medical community and see what their advice is and what they have to offer. If you decide to go the medical route as we did, there are still many

natural things you can do to aid you in healing during and after treatment. Don't think it has to be one or the other; it can be a combination of things as we did, or perhaps it could be the all-natural path as our dear friend Esther and others have followed.

2. Try to find a naturalist/licensed practitioner who has experience dealing with cancer. A good naturalist will be able to guide you concerning your diet and supplements. If you don't have cancer, seek out a holistic health coach who can guide you into a proper diet and lifestyle changes. He or she will work with you daily on improving the quality of your life.

3. Befriend a vegan or vegetarian. They are a wonderful source of information and will have some great recipes for you to try. I included some at the end of this book to get you started. Though you might not cut meat out of your diet completely, adding a few clean meals to your diet will help you.

4. Go with your gut. If something doesn't make sense or feel right, don't do it. Do your own research. Seek out the answers yourself. No matter what the outcome, if you go with your heart, you will never regret it. Educate yourself. Read more natural and holistic books. Explore options outside the medical community. Search out success stories regarding alternative medicine.

5. Invest in companies such as Melaleuca or Amway. We have switched all our household products to a more natural Melaleuca brand. It's just as important to use clean products as it is to ingest clean foods. I believe the reason for much disease and cancer today is due to the increase in pollutants, including those in cleaning products.

6. Make donations whether of blood, platelets, money, or time. Most blood banks are in dire need, and you will literally save lives by donating blood. It's quick and easy; each donation can save up to three lives. Also support organizations such as Michael's Way, Make-A-Wish, and the Ronald McDonald

House. They work so hard to make life just a little easier for those stricken with health crises.

Today, we are living happy and healthy lives. Once we felt stable with Logan's remission, we brought a beautiful baby girl into our family and named her Hope. I get chills just thinking of how special and beautiful her name is to our family. Without having hope through the past years, we would have never made it through. I would say that Hope completed our family, but I just gave birth to another baby girl, Mia, providing Hope a little sister. The boys are just thrilled to be big brothers, and they enjoy showering their sisters with love and attention. We feel so fortunate to finally be back to normal life and just living.

141

CHAPTER 31

GREAT RECIPES

One of hardest parts of getting healthy is finding meals the whole family will eat. Now that you know what you should eat, how do you prepare healthy but yet tasty meals? When I had put out interest on Caring Bridge for some help in this area, I was introduced to Barry and Laure. They immediately sent me many delicious recipes which they had compiled.

Barry & Laure Lovelace are the owners of B&L Fitness, Inc.: operating the Barry Lovelace Athlete Training Academy, Totally Fit Boot Camp, and several athletic training DVD's.

Promoting a 'healthier you' is their main goal. Although they would love the world to be vegan not only for the animals, but for the environment as well, they understand that is not realistic. They help others make little changes in their weekly or monthly diets resulting in a more energetic and healthier being. Many of their athletes and campers have begun a more plant based diet and are feeling incredible.

They actively work with people from all over the world via Skype/Email etc. You can reach them at igetfit@yahoo.com for information on how to change your overall health.

Harvest Burgers   Serves 6

2 tablespoons oil
1 teaspoon ground cumin
1 medium yellow onion, diced

1 red bell pepper, cored and diced
1/2 cup corn (I used vacuum packed, could use fresh or frozen)
1 cup cooked brown rice
1 cup quick oats, lightly toasted (in shallow pan in 350 oven for 5 min.)
1 15 oz. can pumpkin or squash puree (I used pumpkin)
2 tablespoons fresh-chopped cilantro
1 tablespoon balsamic vinegar
1 teaspoon salt and pinch of cayenne pepper + ground black pepper
6 burger buns or large rolls

Heat 1 tablespoon oil and add the onion and cumin; sauté until they begin to brown about 5 min. Add the red pepper, corn kernels and sauté until tender about 3-4 min.
Transfer to a large bowl. Cool for 5 minutes, and then add the rice, oats, pumpkin, cilantro, vinegar, and seasonings. Form into six patties. Heat the remaining oil and brown about 3 minute per side.

Nutritional Info: 310 calories, 9 gm fat, 51 gm Carb, 9 gm Protein, 7 gm Fiber

Red Bean Salad

Salad ingredients:
1 can of kidney beans
5 thinly sliced radishes
2 cups shredded red cabbage

Dressing ingredients:
2 tablespoons red wine vinegar
1 tablespoon Dijon mustard
2 garlic cloves, minced
1 small yellow pepper, diced
1 small shallot, finely chopped
2 tablespoons chopped fresh parsley

4 tablespoons olive oil, pinch of oregano, salt, and pepper to taste

Put salad ingredients together in a large bowl. Mix dressing ingredients very well. Pour over salad and toss well. Enjoy!

Chopped Vegetable Salad

2 beefsteak tomatoes, sliced thick
1 bunch of asparagus
1 large green pepper, top and bottom sliced off
2 ears of corn
3 large carrots, peeled and sliced thick lengthwise
1/4 pound fresh green beans, ends trimmed
2 cloves garlic, minced
1/8 cup balsamic vinegar
1/3 cup Dijon mustard
3/4 cup olive oil
1 head romaine lettuce, washed and sliced thin

In a large bowl add garlic and 2 ounces of olive oil. Add all vegetables except lettuce, season with salt and black pepper. Grill vegetables on medium heat and set aside. In a small bowl combine balsamic vinegar, Dijon mustard, and remaining olive oil until blended. Chop all vegetables into medium pieces. Just before serving add vinaigrette and place on top of shredded romaine lettuce.

"Egg" Nog

1 1/2 cups vanilla soy milk
1 scoop of soy protein powder
1 teaspoon rum extract (optional)
1/8 teaspoon ground nutmeg, pinch turmeric
1 cup vanilla soy ice cream

Directions: Place all ingredients except for ice cream in a blender and blend until smooth. Add the ice cream and blend until creamy. Serves 2

Avocado Salsa

8 ounces frozen corn kernels, thawed
1 (2.25 oz.) can sliced black olives, drained
1/2 red bell pepper
1/2 small onion, chopped
1/4 teaspoon salt
1/4 teaspoon black pepper

Directions: In a large bowl, mix corn, olives, red bell pepper and onion. In a small bowl, mix garlic, olive oil, lemon juice, oregano, salt and pepper. Pour into the corn mixture and toss to coat. Cover and chill in the refrigerator 8 hours or overnight. Stir the avocados into the mixture before serving.

Chili Cornbread Pie

Filling Ingredients: 1 can (15oz) chili beans, do not drain
1 1/2 cups frozen corn
1/2 cup fresh parsley, minced
1 cup red onion, diced
1 teaspoon cilantro, minced

Cornbread:

1 cup cornmeal
3/4 cup flour (I use whole wheat pastry flour)
1 tablespoon maple syrup
2 teaspoon baking powder
1 tablespoon red wine vinegar

1/2 teaspoon sea salt

2 tablespoon safflower oil

2 1/2 cloves garlic, minced

2 tablespoons and 2 teaspoons olive oil

2 tablespoons lemon juice

1 tablespoon and 1 1/2 teaspoons cider vinegar

1/2 teaspoon dried oregano

2 avocados, peeled, pitted and diced

1 cup soy milk (or milk)

Direction: Preheat oven to 375 degrees. In a 10 inch pie plate or casserole dish, combine the beans, corn, onion, cilantro, parsley, and vinegar. In a mixing bowl, combine the cornmeal, flour, baking powder, and sea salt. Mix thoroughly. In a measuring cup, combine the soy milk, oil and maple syrup. Let sit for 2-3 minutes until thick. Pour the liquid into the dry ingredients, and stir until smooth. Pour the batter over the bean mixture. Bake until toothpick inserted into the cornbread topping comes out dry, about 25 minutes.

Spicy Black Bean Chili

2 teaspoons olive oil

1 large onion, chopped

1 large green pepper, chopped

1-2 jalapeno peppers, seeded, rinsed, and chopped

1 tablespoon chili powder

1/3 cup fresh cilantro (optional)

1 teaspoon cumin

1 teaspoon oregano

1 14oz. can diced tomatoes

2 16oz. cans black beans, drained

1 cup corn

1/8 teaspoon cayenne pepper

Directions: Add onion, bell pepper, jalapeno and oil to a large skillet. Cook over medium heat until veggies are soft. (about 5 min)
Add spices, tomatoes (undrained), and beans.
Simmer for 15 minutes. Stir in corn, cook for 2 minutes. Add cilantro and serve.

Black Bean, Corn & Quinoa Salad

1 cup black beans
1 cup cooked Quinoa grain*
1/2 cup chopped green pepper
1 teaspoon sea salt
1/2 teaspoon oregano
1 tablespoon vinegar
1 cup corn, cooked (fresh, frozen or canned)
1/2 cup finely chopped onion
1/2 tablespoon sugar
1/2 cup chopped cilantro
2 tablespoons lime or lemon juice
6 ounces V-8 or tomato juice

In a large bowl combine all ingredients and stir. Chill for 1/2 hour and serve. *Quinoa may be substituted with brown rice, couscous or bulgur.

Oriental Cabbage Salad

1/2 head cabbage (chopped)
6 green onions- tops and bottoms- chopped
2/3 cup sunflower seeds
1 package ramen noodles (withhold seasoning) broken into bits
2/3 cup slivered almonds

Dressing:

4 1/2 tablespoons cider vinegar
3 tablespoons sugar
1/2 teaspoon pepper
1/2 cup salad oil
3 tablespoons sesame seeds
1 teaspoon salt
1 package ramen noodle seasoning

Directions:

Mix all salad ingredients. Set aside. Mix all dressing ingredients. Pour over salad mixture and toss together. Let marinate in fridge for about 4 hours.

Couscous Salad

2 cups vegetable stock
1/2 teaspoon ground ginger
1 cup couscous
1 small red onion, diced
1 small zucchini, diced
1/3 cup raisins
1/4 cup fresh lemon juice
1/4 teaspoon ground pepper
3/4 teaspoon cinnamon
1/4 teaspoon turmeric
1 carrot, diced
1 small red bell pepper, diced
1 granny smith apple, diced
1 1/2 cups chick peas, drained
1/2 teaspoon salt
1 tablespoon olive oil

Directions:

In a medium saucepan, whisk together the stock, cinnamon, ginger, cumin and turmeric. Add the couscous and heat to boiling stirring constantly. Boil for 1 minute. Cover the pot tightly, remove from heat, and let stand for 15 minutes.

Fluff the couscous grains with a fork, transfer to a large mixing bowl and let cool. Add the carrot, bell pepper, zucchini, onion, apple, raisins, chickpeas and toss.

Whisk the olive oil, lemon juice, salt and pepper until well mixed. Pour over the salad and toss well. Cover and refrigerate for several hours or up to 3 days.

Heavenly Smoothie   Serves 2

5 or 6 strawberries
5 or 6 peach slices
1 cup of apple juice
1 banana
Handful of ice

Directions:
Combine all ingredients in a blender and puree.

Good Morning Pineapple Shake   Serves 1

1 banana
8 ounces pineapple juice
1 cup ice
1/2 pkg. (6 ounces) silken firm tofu (mori-nu brand)

Directions:
Combine all ingredients and blend until smooth.

Asian Cabbage and Almond Salad

3 cups finely shredded cabbage
2 green onions, finely sliced
1/2 cup raw almonds, dry roasted

Dressing:
1 tablespoon olive oil
1 teaspoon sesame oil
1 tablespoon lemon juice
1 tablespoon hoison sauce
1 Tbsp. light soy sauce or tamari
1 clove garlic, finely chopped
3/4 tsp. finely chopped ginger (optional)

Directions:
Chop the almonds. Add to cabbage, along with onions. Mix together the dressing and stir desired amount into the cabbage. Refrigerate to allow flavors to infuse the cabbage before serving.

Portabella Burgers

4 Portabella mushrooms (or however many you wish, 1 mushroom = 1 burger) Good quality balsamic vinaigrette dressing (I use Newman's Own)

Directions:
Pour some dressing into a shallow pan. Put mushrooms in with undersides facing down and marinate for a few hours or overnight.

Cook mushrooms on medium-high heat until done (softened). Serve on grilled buns with fixings of your choice.

These are a staple in our house. I often do them without the marinating. Just keep brushing the mushrooms with the dressing as they cook. They are delicious either way.

Bean Salad

1 (15oz) can kidney beans
1 (14.5oz) can wax beans
1 (15oz) great northern beans
1 (15oz) can green beans
1 (15oz) can garbanzo beans
1 sweet onion, chopped
1 green pepper, chopped
1 red bell pepper, chopped
3/4 cup sugar
2/3 cup white vinegar
1/2 cup canola oil
1/2 teaspoon dill weed
1/2 teaspoon rosemary
1/2 teaspoon dried basil

Directions:
Mix beans, onions, and peppers in a large bowl. In a small saucepan, combine vinegar, oil, sugar, and herbs. Stir over medium heat until sugar dissolves. Do not boil. Pour warm dressing over bean mixture and marinate for at least 2 hours in the refrigerator before serving.

Ashleigh Snyder

Black Bean and Corn Salad

2 cans black beans- I prefer organic, rinsed
1 can sweet kernel corn
3-4 tablespoons balsamic vinegar
1-2 teaspoons dry mustard
1-2 tablespoons cumin
1 sweet red pepper diced
1 pepper of your choice,
diced grape or cherry tomatoes
1/2 bunch fresh cilantro leaves torn from stems
salt to taste

Directions:
Rinse beans and drain corn, adding peppers, tomatoes and cilantro before dressing with balsamic vinegar and spices!

Fresh and Fast Gazpacho

3 large tomatoes, quartered
2 large cucumbers, cut in 2 inch pieces
1 rib of celery, chopped coarse
1 small onion, chopped
3 cloves of garlic
1 tablespoon fresh basil
2 tablespoons balsamic vinegar
1 cup tomato juice
2 teaspoons olive oil
1/2 teaspoon salt
1/4 teaspoon pepper

Directions:
Pulse together all ingredients up to basil in a food processor to coarsely chop until desired consistency. Soup will be chunky. Fold in other ingredients. Chill at least 1 hour or overnight. Serve cold.

Harvest Pie

We just love this pie! It's healthy and delicious and easy to make.

3 large potatoes
1 sweet potato (or yam)
2 tablespoon soymilk (maybe more, maybe less)
1 tablespoon margarine
1 1/2 cups of vegetable gravy (recipe below)
3 cups of assorted fresh veggies spices, salt and pepper to taste

Directions:
Basically, this is a pie with no crust and a mashed potato topping. Preheat oven to 375 degrees. Cook and mash potatoes adding soymilk and margarine to make it creamy and salt and pepper to taste. I also like to add garlic! I usually make the gravy by boiling 1 1/2 cups of water and adding 3 veggie bouillon cubes and boil again for 10 minutes uncovered (this makes it thick and gravy like). But you can use any other gravy recipe.

Chop and clean the veggies (I like to use broccoli, asparagus, snow peas, cauliflower and mushrooms). Put chopped veggies in a round shallow backing dish. Pour gravy mixture on top. Spread mashed potatoes over veggies so that a mashed potato cap covers all the veggies. Bake for 20 to 30 minutes, or until the top of the mashed potato becomes crisp and golden. Cool and serve.

Stuffed Portabella Mushrooms

2 teaspoon olive (preferably extra virgin)
1 carrot, peeled and finely diced
1 medium onion, finely diced
1/4 green pepper, finely diced
1 clove garlic, minced
1 teaspoon basil
1 teaspoon oregano
1 cup cooked brown rice
Salt and pepper to taste
4 medium Portabella mushrooms

Directions:
Heat 1 teaspoon olive oil in nonstick pan over medium heat. Add carrot, onion, green pepper and garlic. Sauté until crisp-tender. Stir in basil and oregano.
Remove from heat and combine with rice. Add salt and pepper to taste. Remove stems from mushrooms. Place mushrooms in lightly oiled casserole dish, stem side up. Top with rice mixture, packing down slightly. Brush lightly with remaining 1 teaspoon olive oil. Bake at 400 degrees for 20 minutes.

Roasted Asparagus Salad

1 1/2 pounds fresh asparagus
1 tablespoon olive oil
salt and freshly ground pepper to taste
2 tablespoons vinegar

Directions: Preheat the oven to 350°F. Prepare the asparagus by cutting off the last inch or so of the woody stalk. Place the asparagus stalks on a baking sheet. Brush them with the olive oil and sprinkle with salt and pepper. Roast in the oven for 10 minutes, until the stalks begin to get tender on the outside. (Thin asparagus spears will take less time than thick spears.) Toss with the vinegar and serve.

Olive Tapenade Bruschetta

2 tablespoons pitted and finely chopped green or black olives
1 teaspoon capers
3 1/2 teaspoons extra virgin olive oil
freshly ground black pepper
12 French bread slices
2 cloves garlic

Directions:
Mash the olives, capers, 1/2 teaspoon extra virgin olive oil and pepper together. Toast the bread on both sides in a toaster oven, under the broiler or on the grill. While the toasted slices are still warm, rub them with garlic and drizzle them with the remaining olive oil on one side. Put a dab of the olive mixture on each slice of bruschetta.

Bowtie Pasta with Sun-dried Tomatoes and Spinach

1 package bowtie pasta about 10 sun dried tomatoes, not packed in oil
3 cloves garlic, crushed
3-4 tablespoon olive oil
large handful of fresh spinach
2-3 tablespoons pine nuts (optional)

Directions:
Boil bowtie pasta according to package directions. Meanwhile, soak sun-dried tomatoes in boiling water for about 5 minutes. Remove and chop coarsely. Put olive oil in a heated sauté pan. Add garlic and pine nuts and cook until pine nuts are starting to brown (don't burn the garlic!) Add sun dried tomatoes and spinach, and cook until spinach is

just wilted. Add cooked drained pasta, and mix thoroughly while still over heat.

Tomato Cucumber Salad with Mint

1/3 cup red wine vinegar
1 tablespoon sugar
1 teaspoon salt
2 large cucumbers, peeled, seeded, and cut into 1/2 inch slices
3 large tomatoes, chopped
2/3 cup chopped red onion
1/2 cup chopped fresh mint
2 tablespoons olive oil
salt and pepper to taste

Directions: In a large bowl, combine vinegar, sugar and salt. Mix in cucumbers and marinate for 1 hour, stirring occasionally. Gently toss tomatoes, onion, mint and olive oil with the marinated cucumbers. Season with salt and pepper.

Summer Tomato Salad

1 pint cherry tomatoes, halved
1 pint yellow pear tomatoes, halved
1/4 cup chopped green onions
1 clove minced garlic
1/4 cup chopped fresh basil
1/4 cup chopped cilantro
salt and pepper to taste

Directions: In a bowl toss together all ingredients. Refrigerate 30 minutes and toss again before serving.

Fabulous Fruit Salad

1 red apple, chopped
1 granny smith apple, chopped
1 nectarine, sliced
2 stalks celery, chopped
1/2 cup dried cranberries
1/2 cup chopped walnuts
1 8-ounce container lemon yogurt (I use soy yogurt)

Directions:
Mix everything up and chill until ready to eat. This is yummy and you can put any fruit in it that you want. This time of year I think I would substitute the apples for blueberries and strawberries, yum!

Tortilla-Black Bean Casserole

2 cup chopped onion
1 1/3 cup chopped green pepper
14 oz can stewed tomatoes
3/4 cup salsa
1/2 tablespoon garlic
2 tablespoon cumin
2 15-oz cans black beans, drained
8 corn tortillas
1 1/2 cup shredded Follow Your Heart soy cheese

Directions: In a large skillet over medium heat, combine first 6 ingredients, bringing the mixture to a boil. Reduce heat and simmer uncovered for 5 minutes. Stir in beans. Spread 1/3 of the bean mixture over the bottom of a 13x9 pan.Top that with half of the tortillas, overlapping as necessary and half of the cheese. Add another 1/3 of the bean mixture, then remaining tortillas and bean mixture. Cover and bake at 350 for 30 minutes or until heated through. Sprinkle with remaining cheese and let stand for 10 minutes. Garnish with shredded lettuce and chopped tomatoes. For more of a Mexican flair, add slices of avocado on top or your favorite guacamole.

Greek Chick Pea Salad

This recipe proves that it is not difficult or time consuming to prepare healthy food. This is as easy as it gets and it's delicious. We eat it over salad greens or with pita bread or just by itself.

2- 16 ounce cans chickpeas (garbanzo beans), rinsed and drained
3 plum tomatoes, diced
3 celery stalks, finely diced
3 scallions, sliced thinly
1/2 cup kalamata olives, pitted and chopped
8 basil leaves, shredded
1 tablespoon olive oil
juice of 3 lemons
salt and freshly ground black pepper to taste

Directions:
Combine the chickpeas in a large bowl with the remaining ingredients. Toss well and taste for seasoning. Serve at room temperature or chilled. (This recipe can be made in advance and stored in the refrigerator for up to 3 days.)

Cranberry Walnut Slaw

1 16 oz. package shredded coleslaw mix
1/2 large sweet onion, chopped
1 stalk celery, chopped
1/2 cup dried cranberries
1/4 cup chopped walnuts

1/2 cup white vinegar
1/3 cup white sugar
1/2 cup vegetable oil
1 1/2 teaspoons salt
1 1/2 teaspoons dry mustard
black pepper to taste

Directions: In a large bowl, toss together the coleslaw mix, onion, celery, cranberries and walnuts. Mix the vinegar, sugar, oil, salt, mustard and pepper in a jar with a lid. Pour over the slaw mixture and toss to coat. Refrigerate until serving.

Pumpkin Pie Oatmeal

1 cup water
1/2 cup oats
1/4 cup pumpkin puree
cinnamon pumpkin pie spice
walnuts (optional)
maple syrup

Directions: Boil water and add oats. Reduce heat and cook oatmeal until most of the water is absorbed. Mix in pureed pumpkin and sweeten to taste with maple syrup, cinnamon, and pumpkin pie spice. Top with walnuts.

Vegetarian Stuffed Red Peppers

4 cup cooked wild rice
2 cup dry bread cubes
2 cup cooked/crumbled soy sausage (Gimme Lean) or Boca Burgers
1 onion, diced
2 - 3 stalks celery, diced

2 cup shiitake mushrooms, diced
1 - 16 oz can tomato sauce
4-6 whole red peppers, depending on size, stems and seeds removed
2 cups vegetable broth
salt & pepper to taste
herbs to taste - Italian or sage & thyme

Directions: Saute onions and celery until almost soft. Add mushrooms, cook until all is soft. Remove from heat and add rice, sausage or Bocas, salt, pepper and herbs, mix well. Add bread cubes, mix. Add 1/2 of sauce and all of broth slowly until moist but not too wet (you may need to use a little more or a little less liquid). Spoon mixture into peppers. Put 1/2 of remaining sauce in bottom of pan. Place peppers on top of sauce, pour remaining sauce over peppers.

Cover and bake, until peppers are tender, about 40 minutes at 350 degrees.
Serve w/ sauce from pan poured on top (you may have to add a little water to the sauce to make it more liquid).

Fall Salad with Asian Pears and Walnuts

Vinaigrette:
1 tablespoon finely chopped shallots
3 tablespoons Sherry vinegar
3 taperspoons Olive oil
1 tablespoon honey salt to taste freshly ground pepper

Salad:
12 cups red or green leaf lettuce, torn into bite-size pieces
3 Asian pears, cored and sliced
2 cups red grapes
3 tablespoons chopped walnuts

Directions:
Place all vinaigrette ingredients in a mixing bowl and whisk to combine.
(This can be made ahead and keeps for up to one week) Toss the lettuce,
pears and grapes with the vinaigrette in a large bowl and serve.

Three Bean Chili

2 cans (16oz) Red Kidney Beans
2 cans (16oz) Pinto Beans
2 cans (16oz) Black Beans
1 small yellow onion, chopped
1 small green pepper, chopped
1 can (14 1/2 oz) diced tomatoes
1 can (6oz) tomato paste
3 teaspoon Chili Powder
1 1/2 teaspoon salt
1 teaspoon Garlic Salt
1/2 teaspoon ground pepper
1/2 teaspoon cumin
pinch of cinnamon

Directions:
In a large pot, saute onion and pepper in 1 tablespoon oil until soft.
Add all other ingredients and bring to a boil. Cover, reduce heat and
simmer for 20 minutes.

Bean Salad

1 (15oz) can kidney beans
1 (14.5oz) can wax beans
1 (15oz) great northern beans
1 (15oz) can green beans
1 (15oz) can garbanzo beans

1 sweet onion, chopped
1 green pepper, chopped
1 red bell pepper, chopped
3/4 cup sugar
2/3 cup white vinegar
1/2 cup canola oil
1/2 teaspoon dill weed
1/2 teaspoon rosemary
1/2 teaspoon dried basil

Directions:
Mix beans, onions and peppers in a large bowl. In a small saucepan, combine vinegar, oil, sugar, and herbs. Stir over medium heat until sugar dissolves, do not boil. Pour warm dressing over bean mixture and marinate for at least 2 hours in the refrigerator before serving.

Eggplant Pomodoro Pasta

2 tablespoons extra virgin olive oil
1 medium eggplant (about 1 pound) cut into 1/2 inch cubes
2 cloves garlic, minced
4 plum tomatoes, diced
1/3 cup chopped pitted green olives
2 tablespoons red wine vinegar
4 teaspoons capers, rinsed
3/4 teaspoon salt
1/2 teaspoon ground pepper
12 ounces whole wheat angel hair pasta
1/4 cup chopped fresh parsley or basil

Directions:
Cook pasta as per package directions. Heat oil in a large skillet over medium heat. Add eggplant and cook, stirring occasionally, until just softened, about 5 minutes. Add garlic and cook, stirring, 30 seconds - 1

minute. Add tomatoes, olives, vinegar, capers, salt and pepper and cook, stirring until the tomatoes begin to break down, 5 to 7 minutes more. Divide the pasta among shallow bowls. Spoon the sauce over the pasta and sprinkle parsley or basil on top.

Cool Cucumber Salad

1 medium cucumber, quartered and sliced
1 medium tomato, chopped
1/2 cup chopped green pepper
1/3 cup chopped sweet onion
2 tablespoons lime juice
2 tablespoons red wine vinegar or cider vinegar
3/4 teaspoon dill weed
1/2 teaspoon salt
1/4 teaspoon pepper

Directions:
In a large bowl, combine the cucumber, tomato, green pepper and onion. In a small bowl, combine lime juice, vinegar, dill, salt and pepper. Pour over cucumber mixture; toss to coat. Cover and refrigerate for 15 minutes. Serve with a slotted spoon.

Sweet and Sour Bean and Spinach Salad

1 can (15 ounces) Pinto beans rinsed and drained
1 cup cauliflower florets
1 small avocado, peeled, pitted, cubed
1/2 cup chopped red bell pepper
2 green onions and tops, sliced
3 tablespoons finely chopped parsley
1/2 cup prepared sweet and sour dressing
4 cups packaged salad spinach

1 can (11 ounces) Mandarin orange segments, drained
2 tablespoons toasted sunflower seeds, optional
Salt and pepper to taste

Directions:
Combine beans, vegetables, and parsley in salad bowl; pour dressing over and toss. Add oranges and spinach and toss; season to taste with salt and pepper. Spoon salad into bowls; sprinkle with sunflower seeds.

Open-Face Ratatouille Sandwiches

These are really good. You can top anything, this recipe calls for French bread, but there are other possibilities such as an omelet.

1 small eggplant, cut into 1-inch pieces
1 small zucchini or yellow summer squash, cut into 3/4-inch-thick slices
1 medium red sweet pepper, cut into strips
1/2 of a small red onion, cut into 1/2-inch-thick wedges
1 tablespoon olive oil
1/2 teaspoon herbs de Provence or dried thyme, crushed
1/4 teaspoon kosher salt
1/8 teaspoon ground black pepper
2 medium plum tomatos, each cut lengthwise into 6 wedges
8 small or 4 large 1/2-inch-thick slices whole wheat or white French bread, toasted (about 8 ounces total)
1 clove garlic, halved
2 tablespoons balsamic vinegar

Directions:
Preheat oven to 400 degrees F. Coat a large shallow roasting pan with nonstick cooking spray. Add eggplant, zucchini, sweet pepper, and red onion to prepared pan. Drizzle with olive oil; sprinkle with herbs de Provence, salt, and black pepper. Toss to coat. Roast vegetables for 30 minutes, tossing once. Add plum tomatoes to roasting pan. Roast for 15

to 20 minutes more or until vegetables are tender and lightly browned in spots.

Meanwhile, rub toasted bread with the cut sides of the garlic clove. Place two small slices or one large slice of the bread on each of four serving plates. Sprinkle balsamic vinegar over vegetables; toss gently to coat. Spoon warm vegetables on top of bread.

Jicama-Apple Slaw

This is the perfect 'something different' to offer at picnics and cookouts. It's 100% dairy free, refreshing and nutritious.

1/3 cup packed chopped fresh cilantro, plus leaves for garnish
2 tablespoons chopped fresh mint, plus leaves for garnish
1-2 tablespoons minced jalapeño pepper
1 teaspoon sugar
3/4 teaspoon salt
1/2 teaspoon ground cumin
1/4 cup lime juice
1/3 cup extra-virgin olive oil
1 1-pound jícama
1 tart green apple, cored (not peeled)
2 navel oranges
2 avocados, diced

Directions:
Place 1/3 cup cilantro, 2 tablespoons mint, jalapeño to taste, sugar, salt, cumin and lime juice in a food processor. Process until finely chopped, about 30 seconds, stopping once to scrape down the sides. With the motor running, add oil through the feed tube in a slow, steady stream until the dressing is well combined. Transfer the dressing to a large bowl. Do not clean the processor, but change to the shredding disk. 2. Using a small, sharp knife, carefully peel jícama, making sure

to remove both the papery brown skin and the layer of fibrous flesh just underneath. Cut the jícama and apple into pieces that will fit comfortably through your processor's feed tube. Shred the jícama and apple in the processor. Add to the bowl with the dressing. 3. Using a sharp knife, remove the peel and pith from the orange. Working over the bowl with the slaw (to catch any juice), cut the orange segments from the surrounding membranes, letting them drop into the bowl. Squeeze any remaining juice into the slaw. (Discard membranes and peel.) Add avocados; gently toss to combine. Serve immediately, garnished with cilantro and mint leaves

Homemade Power Bars

1 cup quick-cooking rolled oats
1/2 cup whole wheat flour
1/2 cup wheat and barley nugget cereal (e.g. Grapenuts TM)
1/2 teaspoon ground cinnamon
egg replacer equal to one egg (or one egg)
1/4 cup applesauce
1/4 cup honey
3 tablespoons brown sugar
2 tablespoons vegetable oil
1/4 cup unsalted sunflower seeds
1/4 cup chopped walnuts
1 (7 ounce) bag chopped dried mixed fruit

Directions:
Preheat oven to 325 degrees F. Line a 9 inch square baking pan with aluminum foil. Spray the foil with cooking spray. In a large bowl, stir together the oats, flour, cereal, and cinnamon. Add the egg, apple sauce, honey, brown sugar, and oil. Mix well. Stir in the sunflower seeds, walnuts, and dried fruit. Spread mixture evenly in the prepared pan.

Bake 30 minutes, or until firm and lightly browned around the edges. Let cool. Use the foil to lift from the pan. Cut into bars or squares, and store in the refrigerator.

Cosmic Chocolate Breakfast Smoothie

6-8-oz. frozen blueberries
6-8 oz. frozen cherries
1 ripe banana
2-3 tablespoons flax seeds
2-3 tablespoons maple syrup
1/4 cup cocoa
1-2 teaspoons vanilla (optional)
8 cups baby greens or other leaf lettuce
1-2 cups of red cabbage or watercress

Directions:
Combine 1 cup water with banana, flax seed, maple syrup, vanilla in a high powered blender and blend until the flax seed is ground and mixture is smooth and thick. Add lettuce and other greens and blend, adding more water as needed. Add frozen berries and blend until smooth.

Ginger Garbanzos and Greens

I know that ginger is not everyone's favorite. If that is you, you can make this without the ginger. It's still good, just more of a curry taste.

2 cups garbanzos, in their liquid
1 large bunch collard greens, washed and shredded
1 roasted red pepper, chopped small
1 1/2" piece ginger, minced
2-3 garlic cloves, minced

1/2 onion, chopped
1 cup vegetable broth
2-3 tablespoons cooking oil
1/2 tablespoon curry powder, or to taste
salt to taste

Directions:

In a large soup pot, heat the oil over medium-high heat. Add the chopped onion and saute until translucent and soft but not brown. Add the ginger and garlic and cook stirring for 1 minute. Lower the heat if necessary to keep from burning the ginger. Add the garbanzos and their liquid (canned is fine), and the vegetable broth. Bring to a light boil. Then add the collard greens. Lower the heat and cover. Allow to cook until the greens become soft, about 10 minutes. Add the chopped red pepper and curry powder. Stir well. Cook another minute or two to let the flavors combine. The collards should keep their vibrant green color; otherwise, they may have become overcooked. Salt to taste and serve with pasta, rice, or as a soup.

Sesame Roasted Asparagus

36 asparagus spears
1 1/2 teaspoons dark sesame oil
1 teaspoon low-sodium soy sauce
1/8 teaspoon black pepper

Directions:

Preheat oven to 450°. Snap off tough ends of the asparagus spears. Combine asparagus and the remaining ingredients in a jelly-roll pan, turning asparagus to coat. Bake at 450° for 10 minutes or until the asparagus is crisp-tender; turn once.

Asparagus with Balsamic Vinaigrette

2 pounds asparagus stalks, washed and trimmed
3 tablespoons good-quality balsamic vinegar

2 tablespoons minced red onion
2 tablespoons extra-virgin olive oil
1 clove garlic, minced
1/4 teaspoon coarsely ground black pepper Coarse
salt to taste

Directions:
Blanch the asparagus in lightly salted boiling water for about 3 minutes
or until crisp- tender; do not overcook. Remove from heat and refresh
under cold water; drain well. Arrange asparagus on serving platter or
individual serving plates.
In a bowl or jar, whisk together balsamic vinegar, red onion, olive oil,
garlic, and pepper. Spoon the vinaigrette over the asparagus, allowing
a little to puddle on either side. Sprinkle lightly with coarse salt.

Buddha's Delight with Tofu, Broccoli, and Water Chestnuts

No need for takeout, this simple version of a popular Chinese takeout
dish will work with just about any vegetable.

3 tablespoons low-sodium soy sauce
1 tablespoon dark sesame oil
1 tablespoon rice vinegar
1 teaspoon sugar
1 (14-ounce) package water-packed extra-firm tofu, drained and cut
into 1-inch cubes
5 cups small broccoli florets
1 1/2 cups (1/4-inch) diagonally sliced carrot
1/2 cup peeled, chopped broccoli stems
2 tablespoons canola oil
1 1/2 cups sliced green onions
1 tablespoon grated peeled fresh ginger
2 garlic cloves, minced
1 cup snow peas, trimmed

1 (14-ounce) can whole baby corn, drained
1 (8-ounce) can sliced water chestnuts, drained
1/2 cup vegetable broth
1 tablespoon cornstarch
1/2 teaspoon salt
4 cups hot cooked short-grain rice

Directions:
Combine first five ingredients, tossing to coat; cover and marinate in refrigerator one hour. Drain in a colander over a bowl, reserving marinade. Cook broccoli florets, carrot, and broccoli stems in boiling water 1 1/2 minutes; drain. Plunge into ice water. Drain. Heat canola oil in a wok or large nonstick skillet over medium-high heat. Add tofu; stir-fry 5 minutes or until lightly browned on all sides. Stir in onions, ginger, and garlic; stir-fry 30 seconds. Stir in broccoli mixture, snow peas, corn, and water chestnuts; stir-fry 1 minute. Combine broth and cornstarch, stirring with a whisk. Add cornstarch mixture, reserved marinade, and salt to pan; bring to a boil. Cook 2 1/2 minutes or until slightly thick, stirring constantly. Serve over rice.

Roasted Eggplant Spread

2 medium eggplants, peeled
1 red bell pepper, seeded
1 red onion, peeled
2 garlic cloves, minced
3 tablespoons good olive oil
1/2 teaspoon cayenne pepper
1 1/2 teaspoons kosher salt
1/2 teaspoon freshly ground black pepper
2 tablespoons lemon juice
2 tablespoons tahini
3 tablespoons chopped parsley

Directions:
Preheat the oven to 400 degrees. Cut the eggplant, bell pepper, and onion into 1-inch cubes. Toss them in a large bowl with the garlic, olive oil, cayenne and salt and pepper. Spread them on a baking sheet. Roast for 45 minutes, until the vegetables are lightly browned and soft, tossing once during cooking. Cool slightly. Place the vegetables in a food processor fitted with a steel blade. Add the lemon juice and tahini, and pulse 3 or 4 times to blend. Taste for salt and pepper. Transfer to a bowl and add the chopped parsley.

Roasted Vegetable Burritos

1 medium onion, diced
4-5 garlic cloves, minced or crushed (jarred is fine)
8 oz. carrots, diced (or sliced if using baby carrots)
2 extra large potatoes, diced (approximately 1 1/4 lbs.)
1 green pepper, diced
1 red pepper, diced
2 zucchini/Italian squash, diced
8 oz. mushrooms, coarsely chopped
4 celery stalks, diced
1 can black beans, rinsed and drained (16 oz.--any kind you like will do)
cilantro
salt
black pepper
olive oil
guacamole
1 package tortillas

Directions:
First, clean and chop all vegetables. Make sure that the vegetables are chopped approximately the same size, so they'll cook evenly. Next, preheat the oven to 400 degrees. Place vegetables in baking dishes, making sure they're spread evenly and not too thickly. Mix some olive

oil, Mexican oregano, cilantro, seasoning salt (or regular salt), & black pepper around with the vegetables to coat evenly. Roast in the oven, uncovered, until done to your liking (I roasted mine about 30-40 minutes). Once vegetables come out of the oven, mix with the beans of your choice, & spoon the filling onto warmed tortillas. Season the burritos with whatever you like (we like guacamole). Finally--roll, serve, and enjoy!!

Tossed greens with pasta, fruit and balsamic vinaigrette

4 ounces uncooked spiral pasta
6 cups mixed greens
2 large fresh pears, cored and sliced
1/2 cup sliced water chestnuts
1/2 cup golden raisins
3 tablespoons sunflower seeds or roasted soy nuts

Dressing:
1 teaspoon rosemary or 1 tablespoon fresh rosemary
1/4 teaspoon ground cinnamon
1/4 teaspoon salt
3 tablespoons balsamic vinegar
1/4 cup olive oil

Directions:
To make the dressing, add the rosemary, cinnamon, salt, balsamic vinegar and olive oil in a small bowl. Whisk thoroughly to blend.
Fill a large pot 3/4 full with water and bring to a boil. Add the pasta and cook until al dente (tender), 10 to 12 minutes, or according to the package directions. Drain the pasta thoroughly and rinse under cold water.
In large bowl, combine the cooked pasta, mixed greens, pears, water chestnuts and raisins. Whisk the dressing again briefly and add to the

salad. Toss to coat evenly. Divide the salad onto individual plates and top with seeds or soy nuts. Serve immediately.

Frozen Pumpkin Mousse Pie   10 Servings

Crust:
30 small gingersnap cookies (about 7 1/2 ounces)
2 tablespoons raisins
1 tablespoon canola oil

Filling:
1 cup canned pumpkin puree
1/3 cup packed brown sugar
1/2 teaspoon ground cinnamon
1/4 teaspoon ground ginger
1/4 teaspoon freshly grated nutmeg
2 pints (4 cups), softened vanilla soy ice cream

Directions:
Preheat oven to 350°F. Coat a 9-inch deep-dish pie pan with cooking spray. To prepare crust: Combine gingersnaps and raisins in a food processor and pulse until finely chopped. Add oil and pulse until blended. Press evenly into the bottom and up the sides of the prepared pan. Bake the crust until set, about 10 minutes. Transfer to a wire rack to cool completely.

To prepare filling: Combine pumpkin, sugar, cinnamon, ginger and nutmeg in a large bowl and mix well. Add ice cream and stir until blended. Spoon the mixture into the cooled pie crust. Freeze until firm, at least 2 hours. Let the pie soften slightly in the refrigerator for 20 to 30 minutes before serving.

Pasta with Roasted Tomatoes, Capers and Olives

1 tablespoon olive oil
1 onion, chopped
2 cloves garlic, minced
2 cups whole, canned plum tomatoes, drained
1 tablespoon balsamic vinegar
1 tablespoon capers
1/2 cup halved, pitted olives
1 sprig fresh oregano, or 1/4 teaspoon dried salt to taste
freshly ground black pepper
1/4 cup freshly grated Parmesan cheese
12 ounces whole wheat penne pasta

Directions:
Heat the olive oil in a large skillet over medium heat. Add the onion and cook, stirring occasionally, until soft and translucent, about 5 minutes. Add the garlic and cook for 2 minutes more. Add the tomatoes and balsamic vinegar and cook for 2 more minutes. Transfer this mixture to a baking dish and stir in the capers, olives, oregano, salt and pepper. Place the dish in the oven and roast for 20 minutes. Meanwhile, bring a large pot of salted water to a boil. Drop in the pasta and cook until it is al dente, about 8 to 10 minutes. Drain. Put the pasta in a warm serving bowl, toss with Parmesan cheese and add the tomato mixture.

Spinach and Lentil Soup

1 large onion, chopped
1 cup shredded carrots
1 tablespoon olive oil
6 cups water
1 (16 ounce) jar salsa
1 1/4 cups dried lentils, rinsed
3/4 teaspoon salt

1 (10 ounce) package fresh spinach, torn

Directions:
In a large saucepan or Dutch oven, saute carrots and onion in oil until tender. Add the water, salsa, lentils and salt. Bring to a boil. Reduce heat; cover and simmer for 50-60 minutes or until lentils are tender. Stir in spinach; simmer 5-10 minutes longer or until spinach is wilted.

Awesome Corn Chowder

2 large onions, chopped
8-10 cloves garlic, chopped
2 tablespoons olive oil
1 red bell pepper, ribbed and chopped
3 jalapeno peppers, ribbed and chopped
6 cups water or vegetable broth
3 large potatoes, diced
2 large sweet potatoes, diced
3 corn tortilla shells, cut into strips
2 cups corn (not canned)
salt, pepper, chili powder (or a fresh chili) to taste

Directions:
Heat olive oil in large soup pot (medium flame), then add onion and garlic. Saute until just tender (5 minutes). Add peppers and saute for about ten minutes. Add the water, potato, sweet potato, tortilla shells, and any seasonings you like (salt, pepper, chili powder) and bring to a boil. Reduce flame and simmer uncovered for about 20 minutes. Add the corn and simmer for another 5 minutes or so. If the soup is too thick, add more broth or even add some soy milk.

PROTEIN BARS

1 cup vanilla protein powder
1/2 cup flour (wheat or white, depending on your preference)
2 cups rolled oats
1/2 cup oat bran or wheat bran
1/2 teaspoon cinnamon
3/4 teaspoon salt
1/2 brown sugar
1 cup mix-ins (carob/chocolate chips, dried fruit, nuts, etc.)
1 1/2 cups plain or vanilla yogurt
1/4 cup vegetable oil
2 teaspoons vanilla

Directions:
Preheat oven to 350 degrees. Lightly spray a 9 by 13-inch baking pan and a cookie sheet with nonstick spray. Mix together the protein powder, flour, oats, bran, cinnamon, and salt in a large bowl. Add in the brown sugar and mix-ins.
Combine the yogurt, oil, and vanilla in a separate bowl, stirring well. Add the wet mixture to the dry and mix until thoroughly blended (it will take a while to get it all mixed). Transfer the mixture to the prepared 9 by 13-inch pan, patting it evenly into place with your hands. Bake for 15 minutes, then remove from oven and cut into bars of any size. Place the bars on the prepared cookie sheet about a half an inch apart and bake for another 15 minutes.
Banana-Cocoa Smoothie

3 or more whole frozen bananas
1 tablespoon cocoa
1 rounded tablespoon all natural peanut butter
about a cup of soy milk, milk or almond milk

Directions:
Blend and enjoy!

Pumpkin Pie in a Glass

1/2 cup pumpkin
1/2 cup soy or other milk
1/2 teaspoon vanilla extract
1/2 cup crushed ice
1 tablespoon liquid sweetener
1 teaspoon pumpkin pie spice

Directions:
Blend and enjoy!

Hawaiian Shake

2 frozen bananas (chopped beforehand)
2 pineapple slices
1 cup pineapple juice

Directions:
Blend and enjoy!

Artichoke Pasta with Pine Nuts

3/4 cup pine nuts
1 tsp olive oil
2 garlic cloves, minced
1 cup chopped onions
10 Kalamata olives, pitted, sliced in half
2 cans (13 3/4 oz.) artichoke hearts, water packed, drained and sliced
1 tsp salt-free Mrs. Dash† Lemon Pepper Seasoning

Directions:
Blend 1 ½ cup vegetable broth, 3 tablespoons flour, 6 oz. whole-wheat rotini pasta, cooked according to directions without salt or fat 1/2 cup chopped fresh parsley. In a small skillet, over medium-low heat, toast pine nuts for 4 to 6 minutes, stirring often. Remove from heat and set aside. Spray a large skillet with nonstick cooking spray. Place the skillet over medium-high heat and add olive oil. When oil is hot, add garlic, onions, and olives. Sauté 1 to 2 minutes. Add artichoke hearts and salt-free seasoning. Cook 1 to 2 minutes. In a small bowl, combine broth and flour and add to the skillet. Stir 1 to 2 minutes with a wire whisk until thickened. Remove from heat. Place hot cooked pasta in a large bowl and pour artichoke sauce over pasta. Add parsley and toasted pine nuts. Toss to mix well.

Asian Noodle Salad

8 ounces udon noodles, uncooked (can substitute vermicelli)
4 ounces pea pods, fresh, cut into thin strips
2 tablespoon sesame oil
1 tablespoon peanut oil
2 tablespoon lite soy sauce
2 tablespoon rice wine vinegar
1/2 ounce mushrooms, dried, such as Chinese tree ear, shiitake, porcini, or morels soaked in warm water for 15 minutes, drained and sliced
1 small carrot, thinly sliced
2 green onions, cut diagonally with tops
1 cup bean sprouts
2 tablespoon dry-roasted peanuts

Directions:
Cook the noodles according to the package directions, omitting salt. Thirty seconds before the noodles are cooked, add the pea pods to blanch. Drain the pasta and pea pods. Mix the sesame oil and peanut oil in a small bowl. In another small bowl, combine the soy sauce and

vinegar. Whisk in 2 tablespoons of the oil mixture. Put the hot noodles in a large bowl. Mix the remaining tablespoons of oil mixture into the noodles. Add the mushrooms, pea pods, carrot, onions, and bean sprouts. Add the soy sauce dressing; toss well. Sprinkle with chopped nuts. Serve hot or cold.

Baked Apples

6 medium Golden Delicious apples
1 cup walnut pieces
1/2 cup raisins, or dried cranberries
1/4 cup unsweetened shredded coconut, (optional)
2 tablespoons maple syrup
1 teaspoon freshly grated lemon zest
1/4 teaspoon ground cinnamon
1/4 teaspoon ground nutmeg
1/2 cup apricot preserves
1 1/2 cups apple cider
1 tablespoon earth balance spread or butter
1/2 teaspoon vanilla extract

Directions:
Preheat oven to 375 degrees. Lightly coat a shallow 8-by-12-inch (or similar) baking dish with cooking spray. Core apples all the way through with an apple corer, making a 1-inch-wide hole. Peel the upper third of each apple. Using a sharp paring knife, score the flesh about 1/4 inch deep around the circumference, more or less where the peeled and unpeeled areas meet. With the paring knife angled down, cut a shallow crater around the top of the hole to help hold the preserves that will go there. Set aside while you make the filling.
Place walnuts, raisins (or dried cranberries) and coconut (if using) in a food processor. Chop the mixture fairly well, but not too fine; you want it to remain somewhat textured. Add syrup, lemon zest, cinnamon and nutmeg; pulse several times to combine. Place the apples in the prepared

baking dish and gently press 1/4 cup filling into each cavity. Spoon a generous tablespoon of preserves onto the crater of each apple. Combine cider and butter in a small saucepan; heat over low heat until the butter has melted. Remove from the heat and stir in vanilla. Pour the liquid over and around the apples.

Cover the apples loosely with tented foil and bake on the center rack for 30 minutes. Remove foil and baste the apples well. Continue to bake, uncovered, for 20 to 35 minutes more (depending on the size of the apples), basting every 10 minutes, until the apples are tender throughout. The best way to test them is with a thin bamboo skewer; the slightest bit of resistance near the center is OK because they'll finish cooking as they cool. Let the apples cool right in the pan, basting periodically. Serve warm, at room temperature or cold, with some of the pan juices spooned over each.

Bean Salad

1/4 cup rice vinegar
1/4 cup vegetable oil
1 tablespoon sugar
2 cloves garlic, minced (2 tsp.)
1/2 teaspoon dried oregano
1/2 teaspoon dried basil
1 15-oz. can black beans, rinsed and drained
1 15-oz. can pinto beans or black-eyed peas, rinsed and drained
1 1/2 cups fresh corn kernels
1/2 cup edamame
1 red, yellow, or orange bell pepper, finely chopped (1 cup)
1/2 small red onion, finely chopped (1/2 cup)
1 2-oz. can diced green chilies with liquid
1/4 cup chopped cilantro

Directions:

Whisk together vinegar, oil, sugar, garlic, oregano, and basil in large bowl. Stir in black and pinto beans, corn, bell pepper, onion, chilies, and cilantro. Season with salt and pepper. Refrigerate 1 hour before serving.

Butternut Squash Soup with Caramelized Onions and Apples

1 rib of celery, chopped
1 carrot, peeled and chopped
1 teaspoon olive oil
4 cups butternut squash, peeled and seeded
3 cloves garlic, minced
1 tablespoon fresh oregano, chopped
1 quart low-sodium vegetable stock, more maybe needed
salt and pepper to taste
1 tablespoon curry powder
1 onion, large dice
1 Granny Smith apple, peeled and cored

Directions:

In a soup pot, sauté the onion, celery and carrot in the oil over medium heat until the onion is golden, about 5 to 6 minutes. Add the squash and garlic cooking 5 minutes, stirring. Add the oregano and stock and simmer about 15 minutes or until the veggies are soft. While the soup is cooking, place a sauté pan at medium-high heat with 1/2 teaspoon of olive oil and sauté the diced onions. Cut the apple into a large dice and when the onions are golden, add to the pan, continue sautéing 2 to 3 minutes. Add the curry and cook 1 minute. Remove from the heat, add the dill and set aside. Place all of the cooked veggies (except the curried onions and apple mix) and liquid from the pot in a blender or food processor and blend until smooth. More stock may be needed to adjust consistency. Return to the soup pot and add the curried onion and apple. Simmer for 2 minutes. Season to taste and adjust consistency.

Eggplant Sauté

2 teaspoons olive oil
1 teaspoon crushed garlic
1 shallot diced
4 cups cubed eggplant (1 inch cubes)
salt to taste
freshly ground black pepper
1 tablespoon freshly chopped basil
1 tablespoon freshly chopped oregano
2 tablespoons freshly grated Parmesan cheese, or soy parmesan

Directions:
Heat the olive oil in a 10" skillet over medium heat. Add the garlic and shallot and cook for 1 minute. Add the eggplant cubes, salt, pepper, oregano and basil and sauté with the olive oil mixture until the eggplant is slightly browned and becomes tender, about 4 to 6 minutes. Remove from the skillet, sprinkle with Parmesan cheese and serve.

Grilled Eggplant & Portobello Sandwich

Looking for a vegetarian option for your next cookout? This grilled eggplant and Portobello sandwich is the answer. For extra flavor, top it with slices of garden-fresh tomato and spicy arugula. When I make these I don't use the mayo mixture, instead I brush the bread with balsamic vinaigrette.

1 small clove garlic, chopped
1/4 cup low-fat mayonnaise
1 teaspoon
lemon juice
1 medium eggplant (about 1 pound), sliced into 1/2-inch rounds
2 large or 3 medium Portobello mushroom caps, gills removed (see Tip)
Canola or olive oil cooking spray

1/2 teaspoon salt
1/2 teaspoon freshly ground pepper
8 slices whole-wheat sandwich bread, lightly grilled or toasted
2 cups arugula, or spinach, stemmed and chopped if large
1 large tomato, sliced

Directions:
Preheat grill to medium-high. Mash garlic into a paste on a cutting board with the back of a spoon. Combine with mayonnaise and lemon juice in a small bowl. Set aside. Coat both sides of eggplant rounds and mushroom caps with cooking spray and season with salt and pepper. Grill the vegetables, turning once, until tender and browned on both sides: 2 to 3 minutes per side for eggplant, 3 to 4 minutes for mushrooms. When cool enough to handle, slice the mushrooms.
Spread 1 1/2 teaspoons of the garlic mayonnaise on each piece of bread. Layer the eggplant, mushrooms, arugula (or spinach) and tomato slices onto 4 slices of bread and top with the remaining bread.

Grilled Potato Salad

4 large Yukon gold potatoes, sliced 1/4-inch thick
5 tablespoons extra-virgin olive oil, divided
2 tablespoons grill seasoning blend
2 tablespoons rosemary leaves, 3 sprigs, stripped and chopped
2 navel oranges, peeled and chopped
1 small red onion, thinly sliced
4-5 cups arugula, chopped, 2 bunches
2 tablespoons red wine vinegar

Directions:
Place potatoes in large bowl and toss with about 3 tablespoons extra-virgin olive oil, 2 tablespoons grill seasoning and rosemary. Grill potatoes 4 to 5 minutes on each side. While the potatoes are cooking, combine oranges and red onion and dress with red wine vinegar and

some extra-virgin olive oil. Remove the potatoes from the grill to the dressed oranges and onions, toss to coat. When you grill potatoes they will be slightly drier than when you use other methods of cooking. By adding the potatoes to the dressing while they are hot, they really will soak in the dressing. When ready to serve, add the arugula to the potatoes and toss to distribute.

Marinated Potato Salad

3 pounds yellow and purple potatoes, washed well
3/4 cup celery, finely diced
3/4 cup red onion, finely diced
1/4 cup olive oil
2 tablespoons red wine vinegar
1/4 cup chopped dill
1/4 cup chopped parsley
3/4 teaspoon salt
1/4 teaspoon black pepper

Directions:
In a large pot, cook the whole potatoes in boiling water for 15-20 minutes or until fork tender. Carefully drain, rinse with cold water, and set aside to cool for 30 minutes. When potatoes are cool, cut them into bite-sized cubes. Transfer the potatoes to a large bowl, add the remaining ingredients, and toss gently. Cover and chill for 30 minutes or more to allow the flavors to blend before serving.

Marinated Tofu Sandwiches

1 cup crumbled extra-firm tofu
1 tablespoon tamari
2 teaspoons balsamic vinegar
1 teaspoon vegetarian Worcestershire sauce

1/2 tablespoon olive oil
1 cup tomatoes, chopped (juice squeezed and discarded)
3/4 cup diced yellow bell pepper
1/4 cup diced celery
1/4 cup chopped green onions
3 tablespoons fresh parsley, basil, or dill, chopped
1 teaspoon Dijon mustard
1/4 cup mayonnaise or vegannaise
Salt and freshly ground black pepper, to taste
Sliced bread or pita

Directions:
In a large bowl, combine tofu with tamari, balsamic vinegar, and Worcestershire sauce. Marinate for 15 to 20 minutes. In a skillet, add oil and marinated tofu. Sauté for 8 to 10 minutes on medium-high heat, tossing until lightly browned. Let cool. Place tofu in a large bowl and add remaining ingredients. Spread on bread or in pitas, or serve as a dip with tortilla chips or crackers.

Ravioli & Vegetable Soup

This is really good and the ravioli make it different. We use vegan tofu ravioli, they can be found in the health food section of Wegman's.

1 tablespoon extra-virgin olive oil
2 cups frozen bell pepper and onion mix, thawed and diced
2 cloves garlic, minced
1 28-ounce can crushed tomatoes, preferably fire-roasted
1 15-ounce pkg. vegetable broth
1 1/2 cups hot water
1 teaspoon dried basil or marjoram
1 6- to 9-ounce package fresh or frozen cheese ravioli 2 cups diced zucchini, (about 2 medium)
Freshly ground pepper to taste

Directions:

Heat the oil in a large saucepan or Dutch oven over medium heat. Add pepper-onion mix, garlic) and cook, stirring, for 1 minute. Add tomatoes, broth, water and basil (or marjoram); bring to a rolling boil over high heat. Add ravioli and cook for 3 minutes less than the package directions. Add zucchini; return to a boil. Cook until the zucchini is crisp-tender, about 3 minutes. Season with pepper.

Shells with Salsa Cruda

5 cups seeded chopped tomatoes (about 2 pounds)
1/2 cup chopped red onion
1/2 cup thinly sliced fresh basil
1/2 cup chopped fresh parsley
1/4 cup chopped fresh mint
2 tablespoons extra-virgin olive oil
2 teaspoons balsamic vinegar
1 teaspoon salt
1/4 teaspoon black pepper
1 garlic clove, minced
8 ounces medium shell pasta
1/2 cup shredded sharp provolone cheese (optional)

Directions:

Combine first 10 ingredients in a large bowl; let mixture marinate at room temperature. Meanwhile, cook pasta according to package directions. Add cooked pasta to bowl; toss gently to coat. Divide evenly among 4 plates. If desired, top each serving with provolone.

Spinach and Potato Salad

1-1/2 pounds new, fingerling or red potatoes
2-1/2 tablespoons red wine vinegar

1 teaspoon Dijon mustard

1-1/2 teaspoons agave

1/2 teaspoon salt

Freshly ground black pepper

1/4 cup toasted pine nuts, divided

4-1/2 tablespoons extra-virgin olive oil

2-1/2 cups baby spinach, whole or roughly chopped

1/4 cup fresh basil, julienned

3/4 cup marinated artichokes, chopped (from jar, rinsed and patted dry)

2/3 cup red peppers, finely chopped

1/3 cup pitted kalamata olives, chopped

Directions:

In a large pot of water, add potatoes and a few pinches of salt. Bring to boil, then lower heat and simmer for 12 to 15 minutes, or until potatoes are tender when pierced. Drain potatoes. In a food processor, combine vinegar, mustard, agave, salt, pepper, 1/8 cup pine nuts, and olive oil. While the potatoes are still warm, cut in halves or quarters. In a large bowl, toss potatoes gently with vinaigrette. Add spinach, basil, artichokes, peppers, olives, and remaining pine nuts and mix. Serve warm or chilled.

Thai Lettuce Wraps

2 cups water

1-1/4 cups Jasmine rice, rinsed

1 tablespoon minced ginger

2 teaspoons minced garlic

1/2 cup coconut milk

1/3 cup diced red bell pepper

1/3 cup diced orange bell pepper

1/4 cup sliced green onions

1/4 cup sliced almonds

1 jalapeño, finely diced

1 tablespoon lime juice
1 tablespoon chopped cilantro
1 tablespoon chopped parsley
1 teaspoon salt
1/4 teaspoon pepper
12 large leaves of loose leaf lettuce, green or red-tipped

Directions:
In a saucepan, bring water to a boil. Add rice, ginger, and garlic. Stir, cover, reduce heat, and simmer for 10 to 12 minutes or until all of the liquid is absorbed. Transfer cooked rice to a bowl and fluff with a fork. Add the remaining ingredients, except the lettuce leaves, and stir well to combine. Place 1/3 cup of the rice mixture in the center of each lettuce leaf, folding the sides of each leaf toward the center. Starting from the stem end of the leaf, roll to enclose the filling, and place seam side down on a platter. Repeat for the remaining lettuce leaves

Tomato-&-Olive-Stuffed Portobello Caps

2/3 cup chopped plum tomatoes
1/2 cup shredded part-skim mozzarella cheese
1/4 cup chopped Kalamata olives
1 teaspoon minced garlic
2 teaspoons extra-virgin olive oil, divided •
1/2 teaspoon finely chopped fresh rosemary, or 1/8 teaspoon dried
1/8 teaspoon freshly ground pepper
4 Portobello mushroom caps, 5 inches wide
2 tablespoons lemon juice
2 teaspoons reduced-sodium soy sauce

Directions:
Combine tomatoes, cheese, olives, garlic, 1 teaspoon oil, rosemary and pepper in a small bowl. Preheat grill to medium. Discard mushroom stems. Remove brown gills from the undersides of the caps using a

spoon; discard gills. Mix the remaining 1 teaspoon oil, lemon juice and soy sauce in a small bowl. Brush the mixture over both sides of the caps. Oil a grill rack (see Tip). Place the caps on the rack, stem sides down, cover and grill until soft, about 5 minutes per side. Remove from the grill and fill with the tomato mixture. Return to the grill, cover, and cook until the cheese is melted, about 3 minutes more.

Vegetarian Taco Salad

2 tablespoons extra-virgin olive oil
1 large onion, chopped
1 1/2 cups fresh corn kernels or frozen, thawed
4 large tomatoes
1 1/2 cups cooked long-grain brown rice
1 15-ounce can black, kidney or pinto beans, rinsed
1 tablespoon chili powder
1 1/2 teaspoons dried oregano, divided
1/4 teaspoon salt
1/2 cup chopped fresh cilantro
1/3 cup prepared salsa
2 cups shredded iceberg or romaine lettuce
1 cup shredded pepper Jack cheese (we skip the cheese and use guacamole instead)
2 1/2 cups coarsely crumbled tortilla chips
Lime wedges for garnish

Directions:
Heat oil in a large nonstick skillet over medium heat. Add onion and corn; cook, stirring, until the onion begins to brown, about 5 minutes. Coarsely chop 1 tomato. Add it to the pan along with rice, beans, chili powder, 1 teaspoon oregano and 1/4 teaspoon salt. Cook, stirring frequently, until the tomato cooks down, about 5 minutes. Let cool slightly. Coarsely chop the remaining 3 tomatoes. Combine with cilantro, salsa and the remaining 1/2 teaspoon oregano in a medium

bowl. Toss lettuce in a large bowl with the bean mixture, half the fresh salsa and 2/3 cup cheese. Serve sprinkled with tortilla chips and the remaining cheese, passing lime wedges and the remaining fresh salsa at the table.

White Bean Salad

1 teaspoon finely grated lemon zest
1/3 cup lemon juice
3 tablespoons extra virgin olive oil
2 tablespoons fresh oregano, minced
2 tablespoons fresh sage, minced
1 teaspoon black pepper
1/2 teaspoon salt
2 15-ounce cans cannellini beans, rinsed
12 cherry tomatoes, quartered
1 cup finely diced celery

Directions:
Combine lemon zest, lemon juice, oil, oregano, sage, pepper and salt in a large bowl and whisk. Add beans, tomatoes and celery, toss and serve.

Rice, Zucchini, and Corn Salad

3 cups cooked brown rice
1 pound small zucchini, cut in half lengthwise and sliced into half moons
2 cups cooked fresh, frozen, or canned corn
1/4 cup thinly sliced green onions
3 tablespoons fresh lemon juice
2 tablespoons extra-virgin olive oil
2 teaspoons Dijon mustard
2 teaspoons dried dill weed
½ teaspoon salt

Directions:
Combine rice, zucchini, corn, and green onions in a large bowl. Whisk together remaining ingredients. Pour over rice and vegetables and toss well. Serve.

Baked Banana and Pineapple Bites

1/2 cup coconut milk
2 tablespoons dark rum
1/2 cup shredded coconut, lightly chopped
2 tablespoons sugar
1/2 teaspoon ground cinnamon
2 firm Bananas, cut into 1-inch diagonal slices
1 quarter fresh Pineapple, peeled, cut into 1/2-inch slices

Directions:
Preheat oven to 400°F. Spray 15x10-inch jelly roll pan with nonstick cooking spray. Stir together coconut milk and rum. In separate bowl, stir together coconut, sugar and cinnamon. Dip banana and pineapple slices into coconut mixture; place on prepared pan. Bake 8 to 10 minutes or until brown and crisp. Serve hot.

Curried Cashews

These are great for having around in bowls during holiday gathering.

6 tablespoons lemon juice
6 tablespoons curry powder
4 teaspoons kosher salt
6 cups unsalted cashews

Directions:
Position racks in the upper and lower thirds of oven; preheat to 250degrees. Whisk lemon juice, curry powder and salt in a large bowl. Add cashews; toss to coat. Divide between 2 large rimmed baking sheets; spread in an even layer. Bake, stirring every 15 minutes, until dry, about 45 minutes. Let cool completely. Store in an airtight container.

Fajitas

1/4 cup olive oil
1/4 cup red wine vinegar
1 teaspoon dried oregano
1 teaspoon chili powder
garlic salt to taste
salt and pepper to taste
1 teaspoon white sugar
2 small zucchini, julienned
2 medium small yellow squash, julienned
1 large onion, sliced
1 green bell pepper, cut into thin strips
1 red bell pepper, cut into thin strips
2 tablespoons olive oil
1 (8.75 ounce) can whole kernel corn, drained
1 (15 ounce) can black beans, drained

Directions:
In a large bowl combine olive oil, vinegar, oregano, chili powder, garlic salt, salt,
pepper and sugar. To the marinade add the zucchini, yellow squash, onion, green pepper and red pepper. Marinate vegetables in the refrigerator for at least 30 minutes, but not more than 24 hours. Heat oil in a large skillet over medium-high heat. Drain the vegetables and sauté until tender, about 10 to 15 minutes. Stir in the corn and beans; increase the heat to high for 5 minutes, to brown vegetables.

Roasted Vegetables

1 small butternut squash, cubed
2 red bell peppers, seeded and diced
1 sweet potato, peeled and cubed
3 Yukon Gold potatoes, cubed
1 red onion, quartered
1 tablespoon chopped fresh thyme
2 tablespoons chopped fresh rosemary
1/4 cup olive oil
2 tablespoons balsamic vinegar
salt and freshly ground black pepper

Directions:
Preheat oven to 475 degrees F (245 degrees C). In a large bowl, combine the squash, red bell peppers, sweet potato, and Yukon Gold potatoes. Separate the red onion quarters into pieces, and add them to the mixture. In a small bowl, stir together thyme, rosemary, olive oil, vinegar, salt, and pepper. Toss with vegetables until they are coated. Spread evenly on a large roasting pan. Roast for 35 to 40 minutes in the preheated oven, stirring every 10 minutes, until vegetables are cooked through and browned.

Blueberry Corncakes

1 1/4 cups whole wheat pastry flour, divided
3/4 cup cornmeal
1 1/4 teaspoon baking powder
1/2 teaspoon baking soda
1/4 teaspoon sea salt
1 1/3 cups almond milk or soy milk
1/2 cup apple juice or water
10 oz. fresh or frozen blueberries safflower oil

Directions:
Place 2 tablespoons of the whole wheat pastry flour in a medium bowl and set aside. In a large bowl, place the remaining whole wheat pastry flour, cornmeal, baking powder, baking soda, and salt, and stir well to combine. In a small bowl, place the soy milk and apple juice, and whisk well to combine. Add the wet ingredients to the dry ingredients and stir until just mixed. Place the blueberries in the medium bowl with the reserved whole wheat pastry flour and gently toss to thoroughly coat the blueberries with the flour. Gently fold the blueberries into the batter. Using a little safflower oil, lightly oil a large non-stick skillet (or griddle), and place it over medium heat. Using a 1/4 cup measuring cup, portion the batter into the hot skillet, and cook until the corncakes have bubbles on top and the edges are slightly dry, about 3 minutes. Using a spatula, carefully flip over the corncakes and cook an additional 2-3 minutes or until golden brown. Serve the corncakes with your choice of fresh fruit or pure maple syrup.

Brown Rice Salad with Citrus-Thai Basil Vinaigrette

2 cups cooked brown rice
2 carrots, grated
1 cup pea pods, thinly sliced on an angle
1 small red onion, halved and minced
6 green onions, thinly sliced on an angle
Citrus-Thai Basil Vinaigrette, recipe below

Directions:
Combine rice and vegetables in a large bowl. Add the vinaigrette and stir to combine. Let the salad sit at room temperature for 30 minutes before serving.

Citrus-Thai Basil Vinaigrette:

3/4 cup orange juice
1/4 cup lime juice
1/2 cup fresh Thai basil leaves, chopped (substitute regular basil or mint leaves if needed)
1 cup fresh cilantro leaves
1 teaspoon salt
1/4 teaspoon freshly ground black pepper
1 heaping tablespoon honey
1/2 cup canola oil
Combine all ingredients in a blender and blend for 1 minute

Perfect Oatmeal   Serves 2

2-1/4 cups water
dash salt
1 cup regular rolled oats
1/2 teaspoon cinnamon
1/4 cup dried cranberries
1/4 cup chopped walnuts
1 tablespoon flaxseeds
1 tablespoon blackstrap molasses

1 cup milk, soy milk or almond milk (I suggest almond milk; it gives this oatmeal even more flavor and nutrients)

Directions:
Combine the water and salt in a small saucepan and turn the heat to high. When the water boils, turn the heat to low, add oatmeal, and cook, stirring, until the water is just absorbed, about 5 minutes. Add cinnamon, cranberries, walnuts, and flaxseeds. Stir, cover the pan, and turn off heat. Let set for 5 minutes. Serve with milk and molasses.

Ultra Thick Shake

4 cups frozen bananas, cut into 2-inch chunks
1 cup almond milk or soy milk
3 tablespoons cocoa powder
2 tablespoon maple syrup
1 teaspoon vanilla

Directions:
Remove the frozen banana chunks from the freezer and allow them to thaw for 5-10 minutes to soften slightly. Place the banana chunks in a blender, along with the remaining ingredients, and process for 2-3 minutes to thoroughly puree and blend flavors. Serve immediately.

Options: add additional almond or soy milk if you desire a thinner shake, or add almond or peppermint extract to vary the flavor, or add a little nut butter of choice for added flavor and creaminess.

Almond Flax Granola

4 cups rolled oats
1 cup raw wheat germ
1 cup sliced almonds
1 cup raw sunflower seeds
1/2 cup flax seeds
1 1/2 teaspoons cinnamon
1 1/2 teaspoons ground ginger
1/4 teaspoon ground nutmeg
1/2 cup apple juice
1/4 cup blackstrap molasses
1/4 cup safflower oil
1 teaspoon vanilla
1 teaspoon almond extract

Directions:
Line two cookie sheets with pieces of parchment paper and set aside. In a large bowl, place the rolled oats, wheat germ, almonds, sunflower seeds, flax seeds, cinnamon, ginger, and nutmeg, and toss well to combine. In a small bowl, place the remaining ingredients, and stir well to combine. Pour the wet ingredients over the dry ingredients and stir well to thoroughly moisten the dry ingredients. Transfer the granola mixture to the prepared cookie sheets, evenly dividing it between the two pans, and spreading it to form a single layer. Bake at 300 degrees for 20 minutes.

Remove the cookie sheets from the oven, stir the granola mixture, spread it out to form a single layer again, and bake the granola mixture an additional 20 minutes. Remove the cookie sheets from the oven, stir the granola mixture, spread it out to form a single layer again, switch the placement of the cookie sheets on the racks, and bake the granola mixture an additional 20 minutes. Repeat the stirring and spreading procedure, as needed, until the granola mixture is dry and golden brown. Remove the cookie sheets from the oven and set the granola aside to cool completely. Transfer the granola to an airtight container and can store at room temperature for 4-6 weeks.

Cashew Spread

1/2 cup cashew butter
2/3 cup vanilla soy yogurt
2 teaspoons agave
1/8 teaspoon salt
1/8 teaspoon ground cinnamon

Directions:
In a food processor, add all ingredients and purée until smooth. Serve with fresh fruit, bagels, or rice crackers.

Garbanzo Tomato Pasta Soup

3 (14.5 ounce) cans vegetable broth
3/4 cup small seashell pasta
1 tablespoon olive oil
1 onion, chopped
2 cloves garlic, minced
1 (15 ounce) can garbanzo beans, drained and rinsed
1 (28 ounce) can whole peeled tomatoes, chopped, juice reserved
1/2 teaspoon dried basil
1/2 teaspoon dried thyme
salt and pepper to taste

Directions:
Bring vegetable broth to a boil in a large pot. Add pasta and cook for 8 to 10 minutes or until al dente. Meanwhile, heat oil in a small skillet over medium heat. Sauté onions and garlic until translucent. Stir into pasta and add garbanzo beans, tomatoes, basil, thyme, salt and pepper. Heat through and serve.

Mango Shake

2 cups almond milk
1 medium fresh mango, pitted
1 medium banana
2 ice cubes

Directions:
Blend it all up and serve!

Kalamata Olive Tapenade

3 cloves garlic, peeled
1 cup pitted kalamata olives
2 tablespoons capers

3 tablespoons chopped fresh parsley

2 tablespoons lemon juice

2 tablespoons olive oil

salt and pepper to taste

Directions:

Place the garlic cloves into a blender or food processor; pulse to mince. Add the olives, capers, parsley, lemon juice, and olive oil Blend until everything is finely chopped. Season to taste with salt and pepper.

Veggie Brown Rice Wraps

1 medium sweet red or green pepper, diced

1 cup sliced fresh mushrooms

1 tablespoon olive oil

2 garlic cloves, minced

2 cups cooked brown rice

1 can (16 ounces) black or pinto beans, rinsed and drained

1 cup frozen corn, thawed

1/4 cup chopped green onions

1/2 teaspoon ground cumin

1/2 teaspoon pepper

1/4 teaspoon salt

6 tortillas (8 inches), room temperature

1/2 cup shredded reduced-fat cheddar cheese (optional OR you can use Daiya Brand dairy free cheese like we doJ)

3/4 cup salsa

Directions:

In a large nonstick skillet, saute red pepper and mushrooms in oil until tender. Add garlic; cook 1 minute longer. Add the rice, beans, corn, green onions, cumin, pepper and salt. Cook and stir for 4-6 minutes or until heated through. Spoon 3/4 cup onto each tortilla. Sprinkle with cheese; drizzle with salsa. Fold sides of tortilla over filling; serve immediately. Yield: 6 servings

About the Author

My name is Ashleigh Snyder. I am a mother of four amazing children; I faced a mother's worst fear—outliving a child—when my son Logan was diagnosed with a rare and aggressive pediatric cancer when he was only fifteen months old. I wrote this story to share hope with others and open their eyes to an alternative method of healing. God chose me to be Logan's mommy, and I want to share this miracle with you.